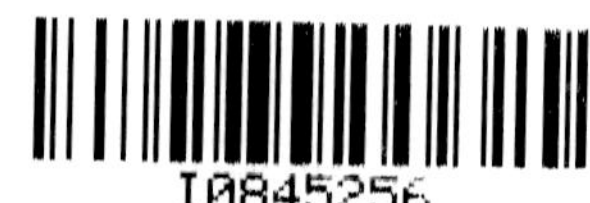

ISBN: 9798862773545

www.facebook.com/DeaBernadette
Instagram: dea_bernadette

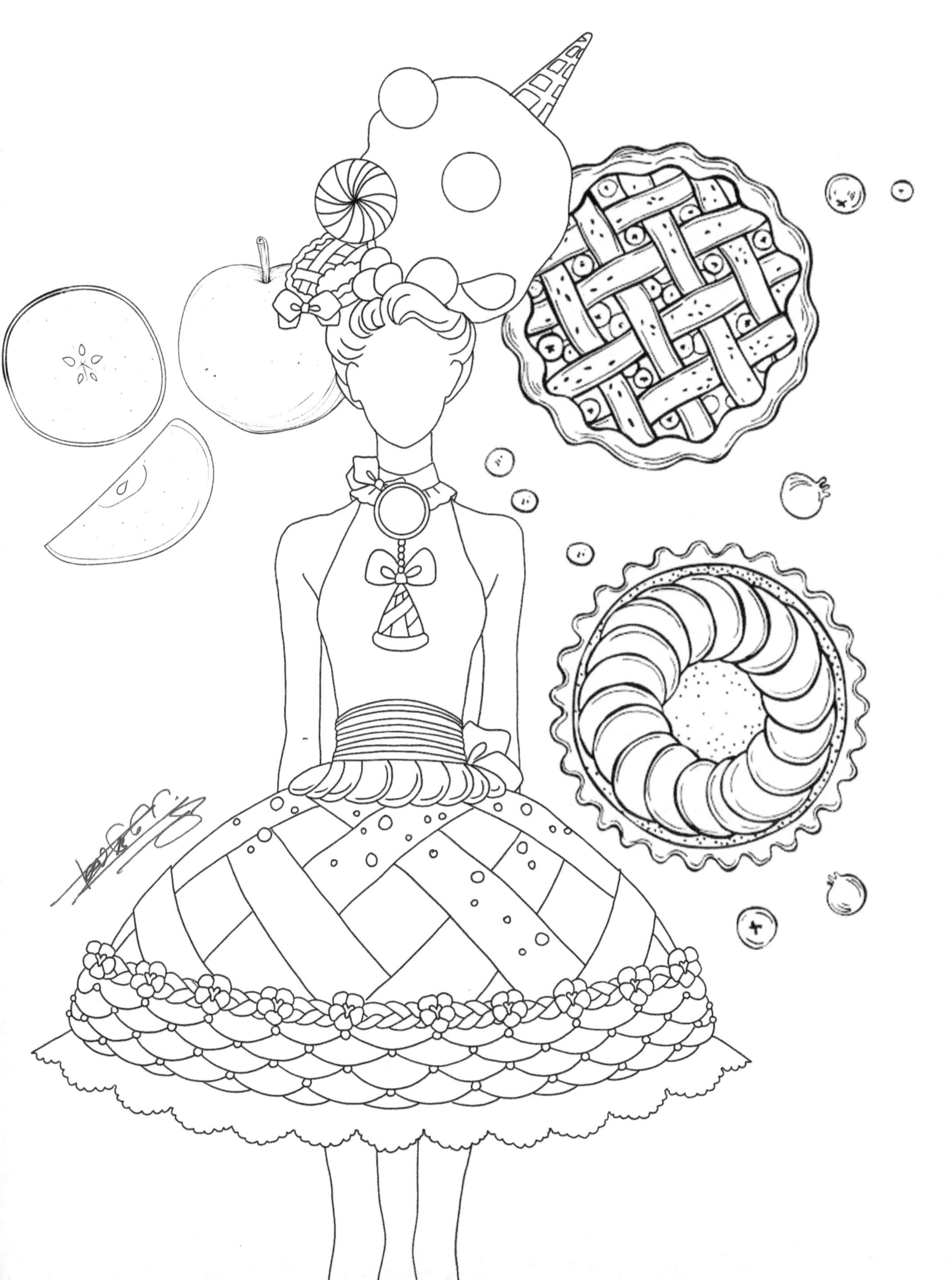

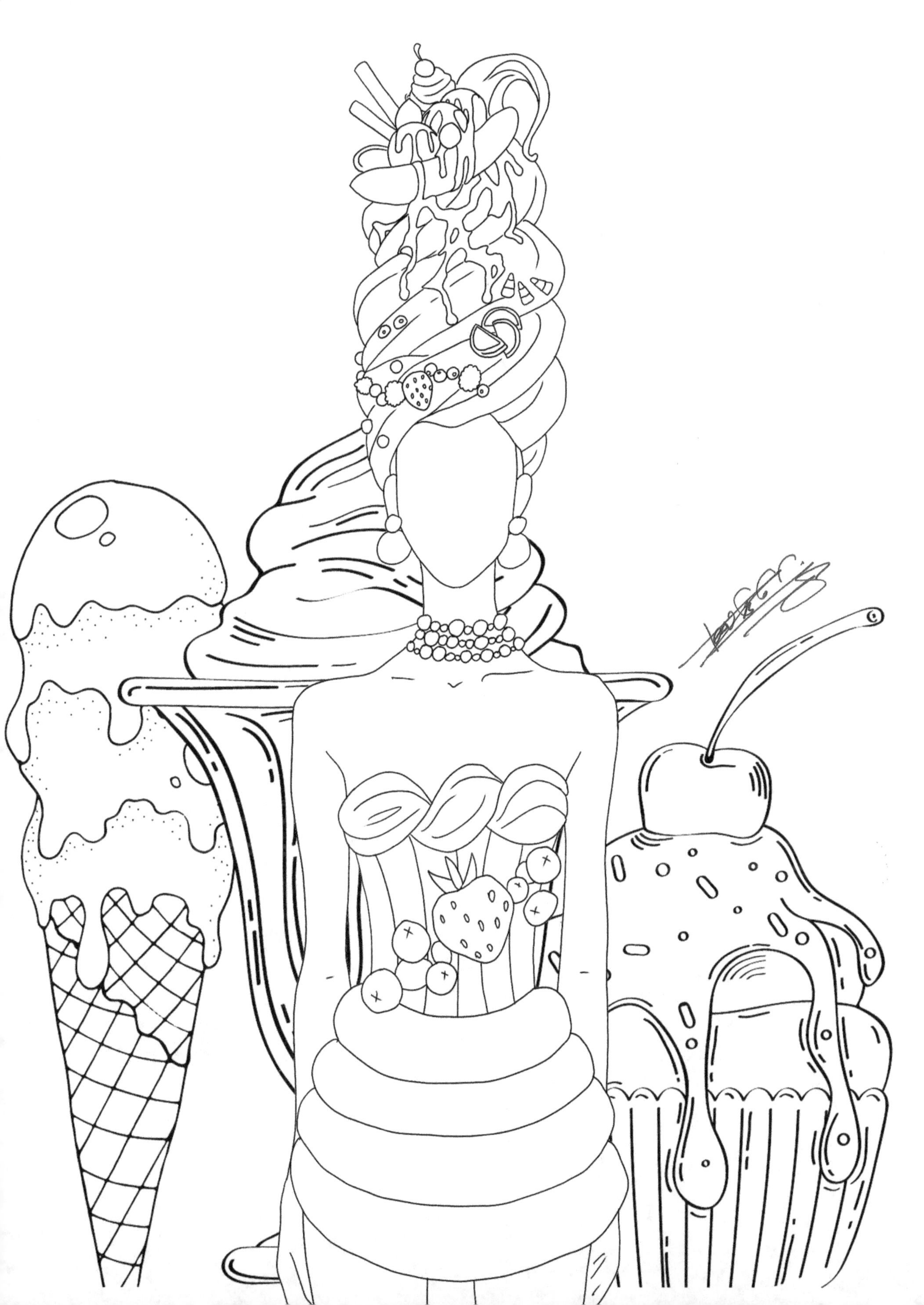

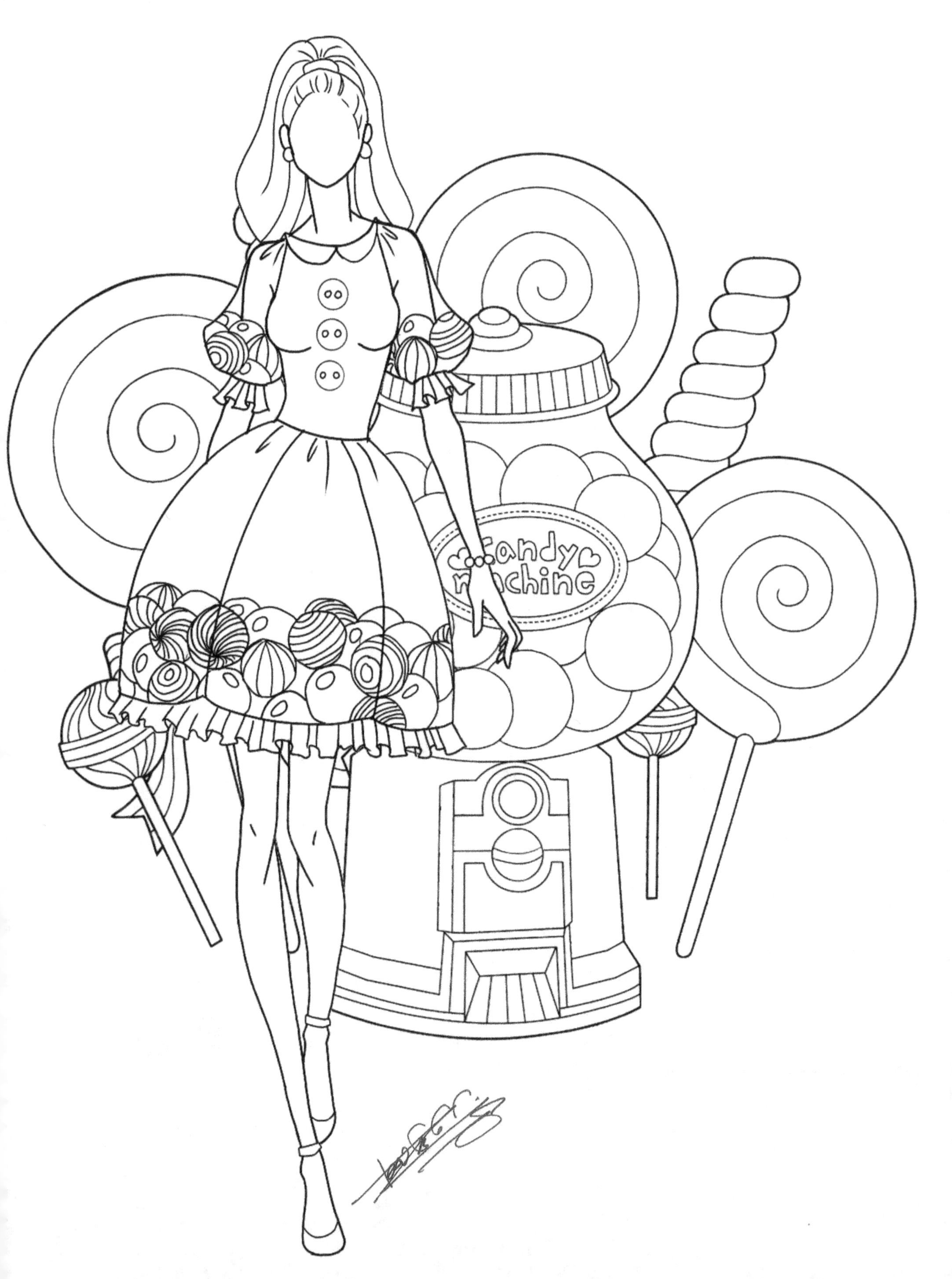

andy
machine

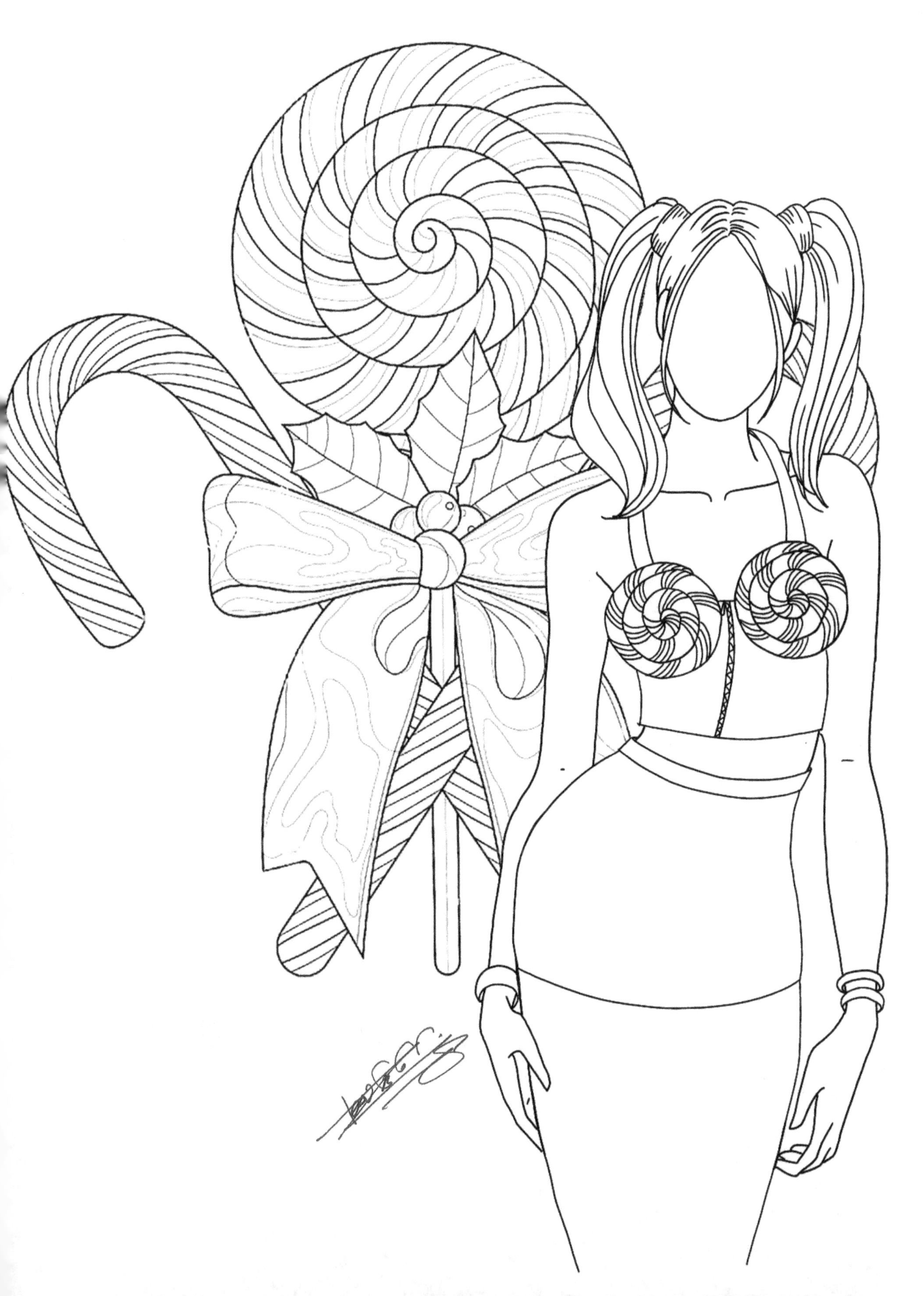

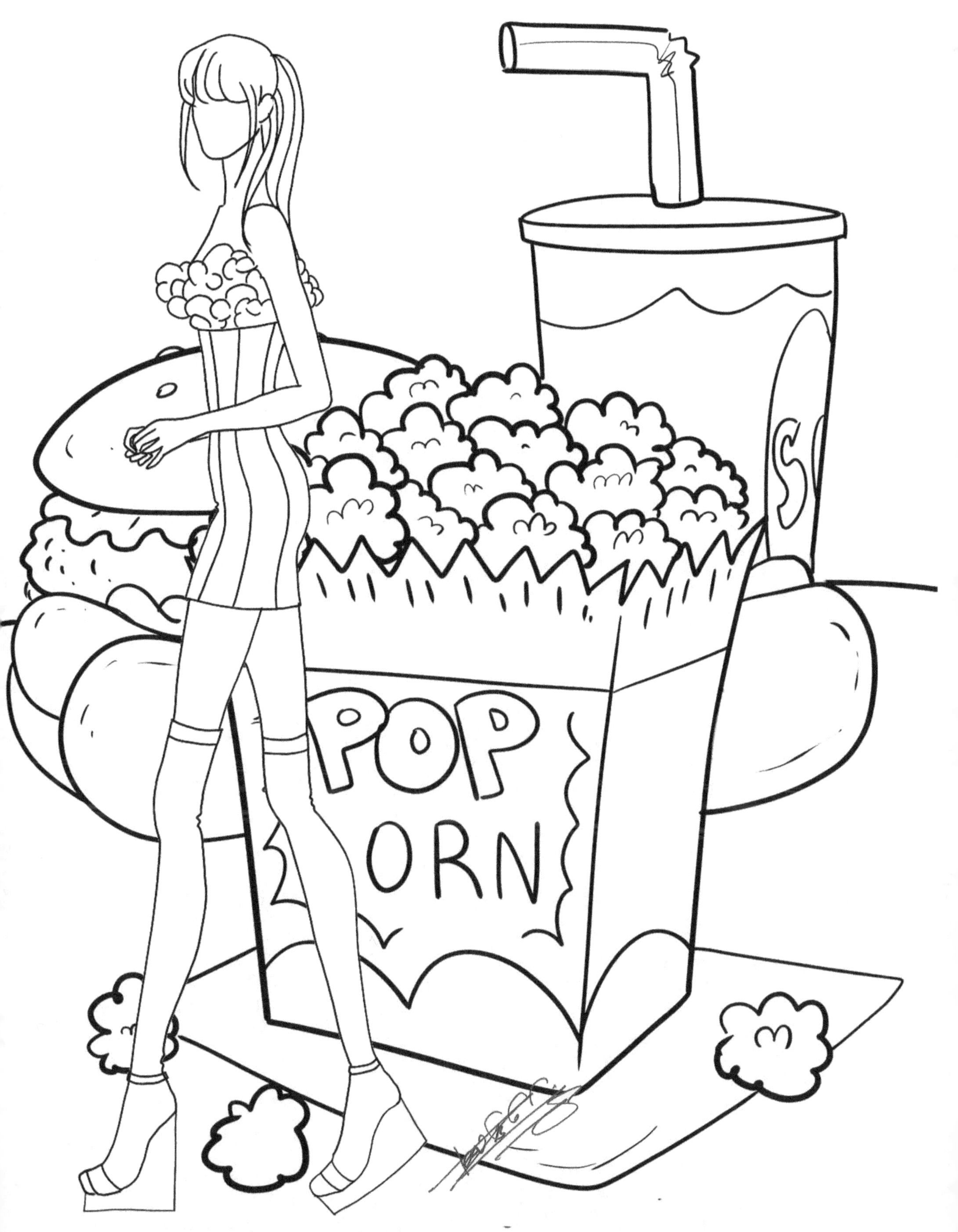

POP
ORN

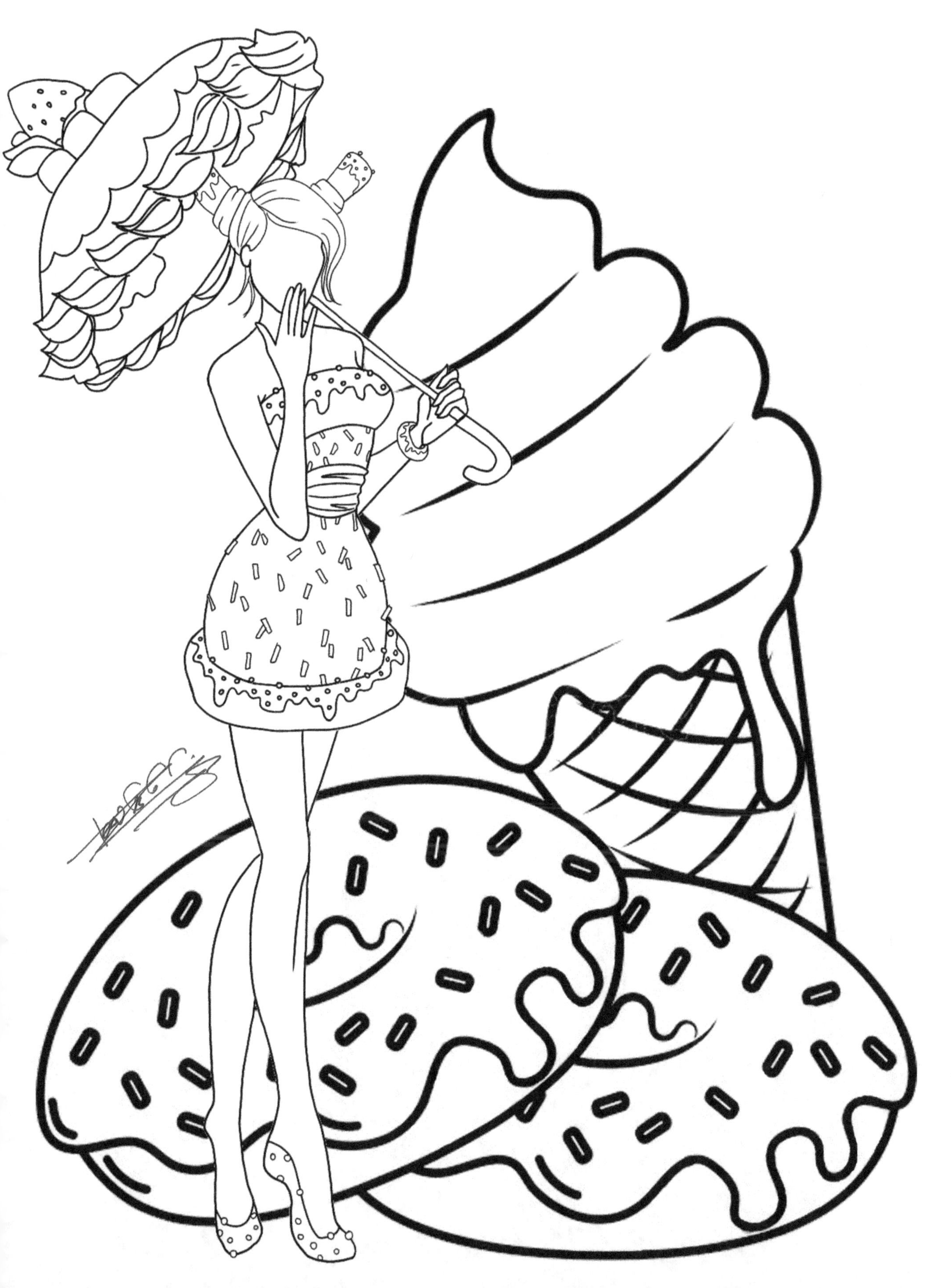

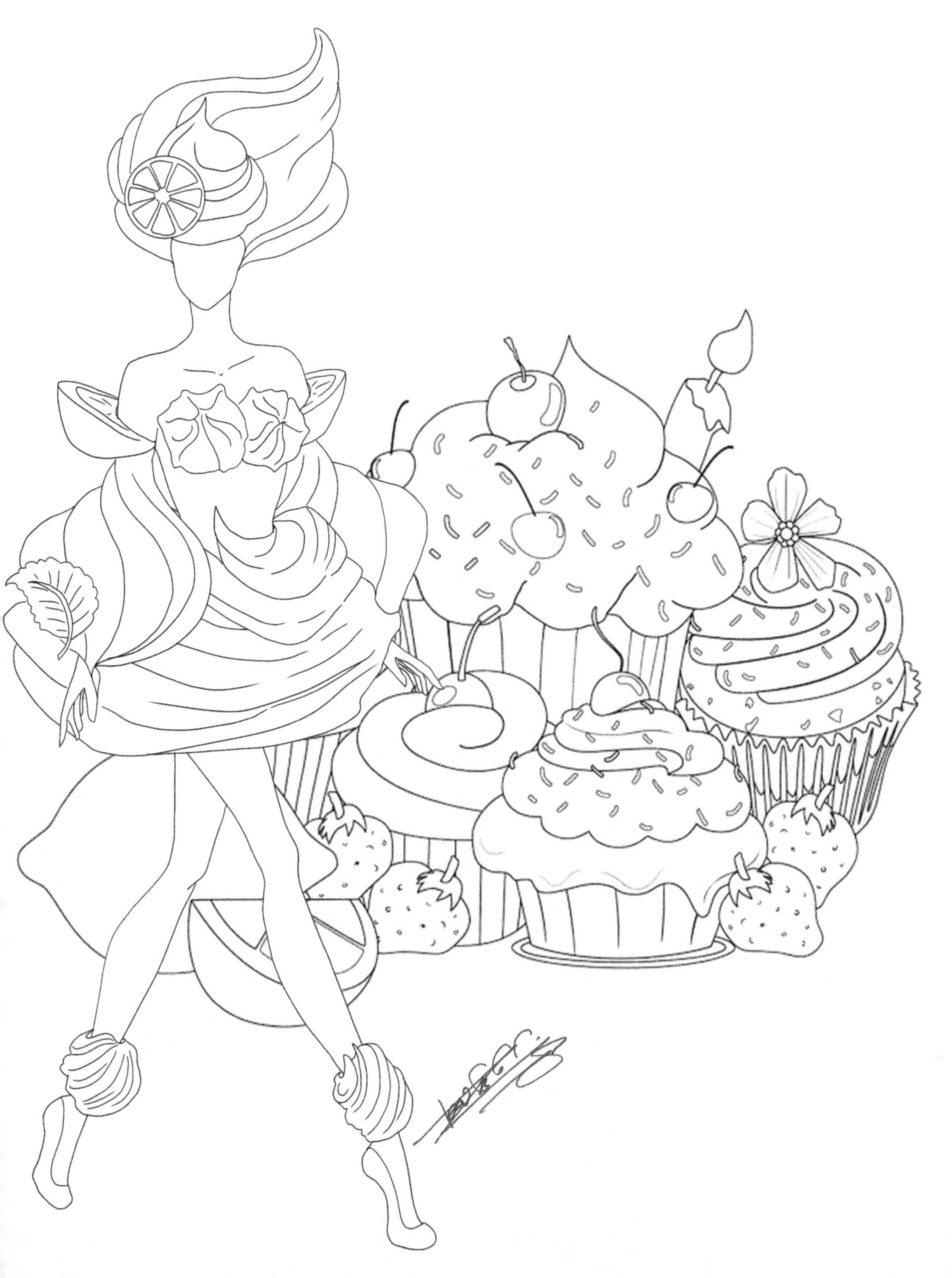

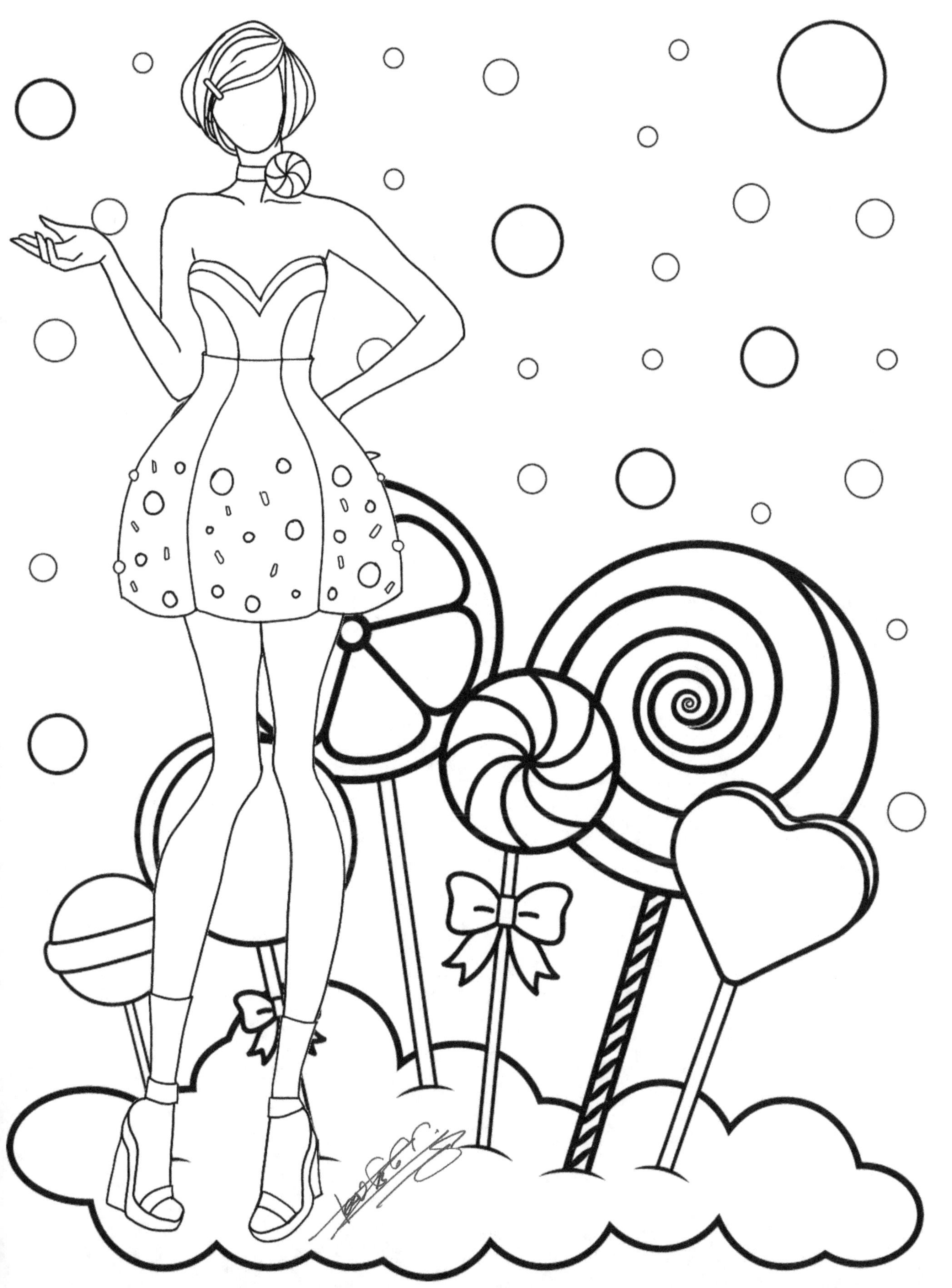

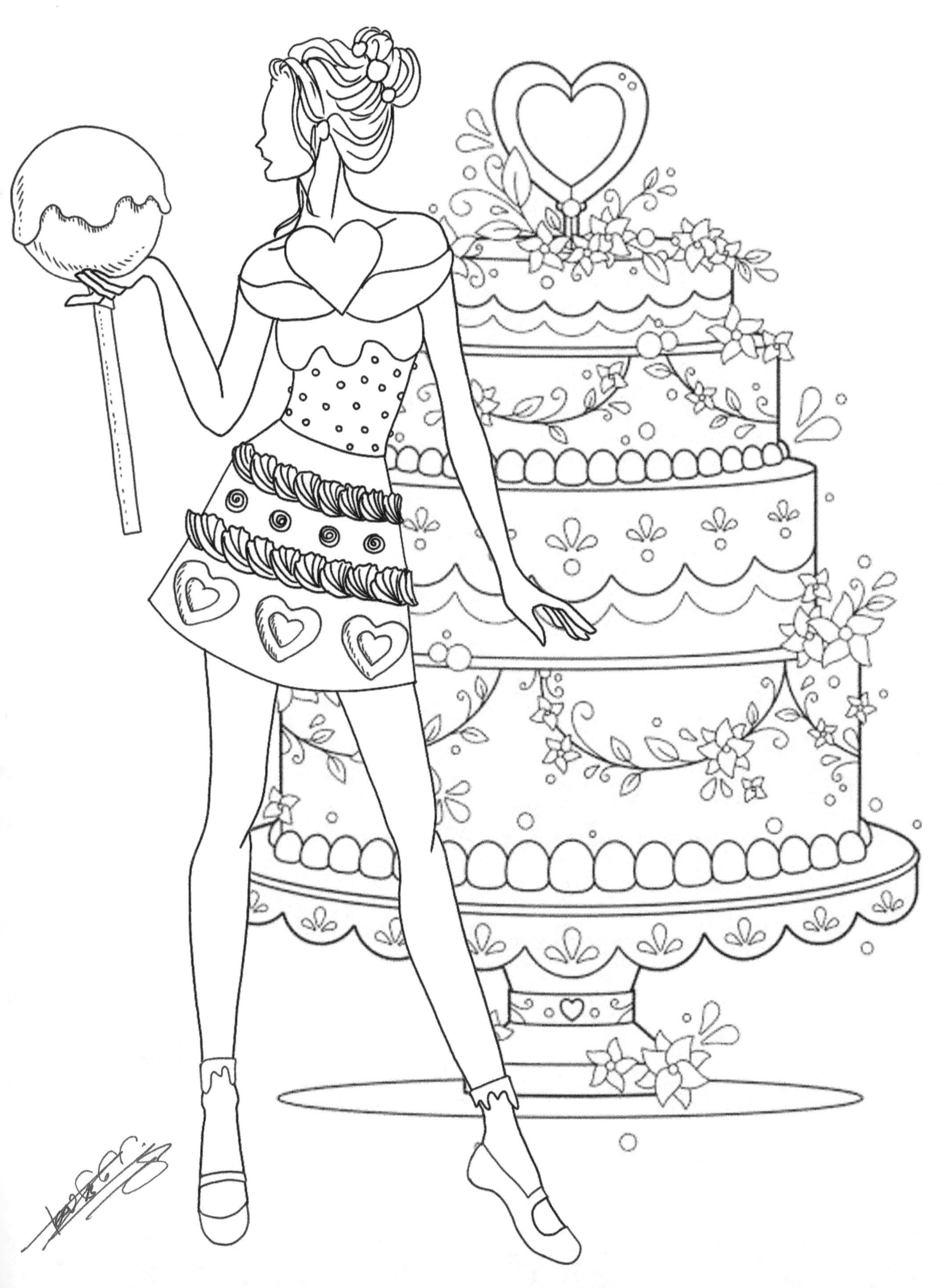

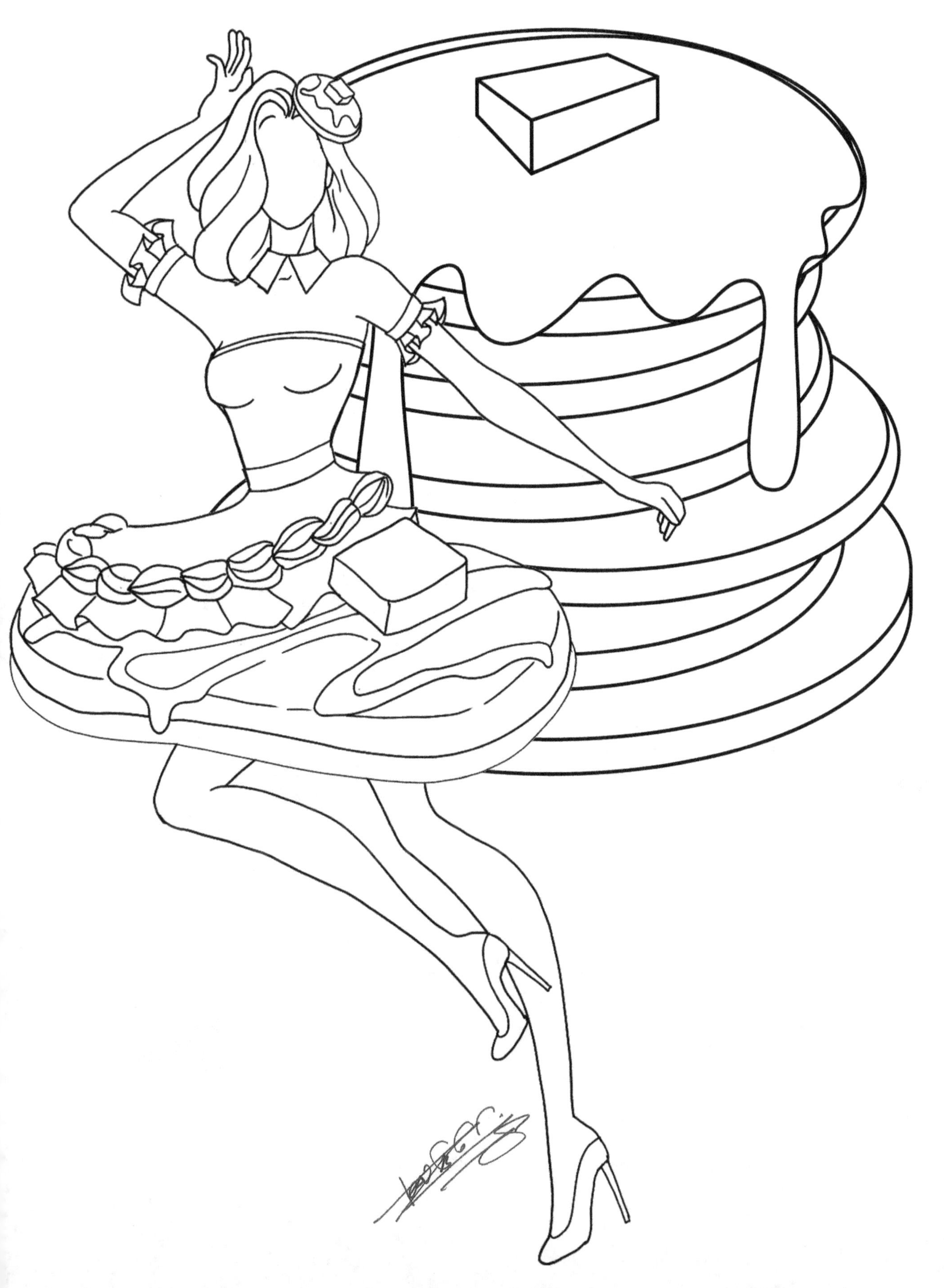

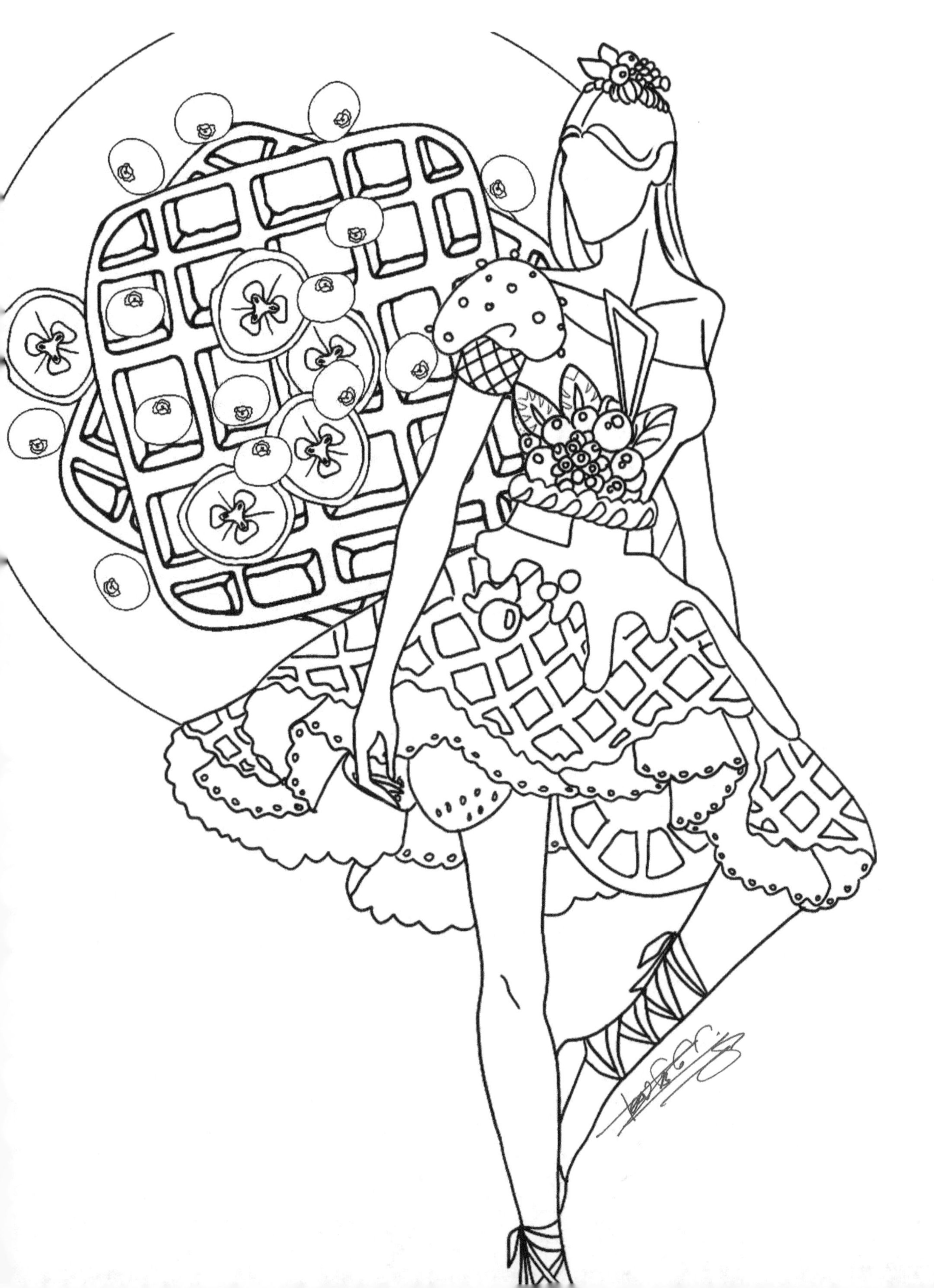

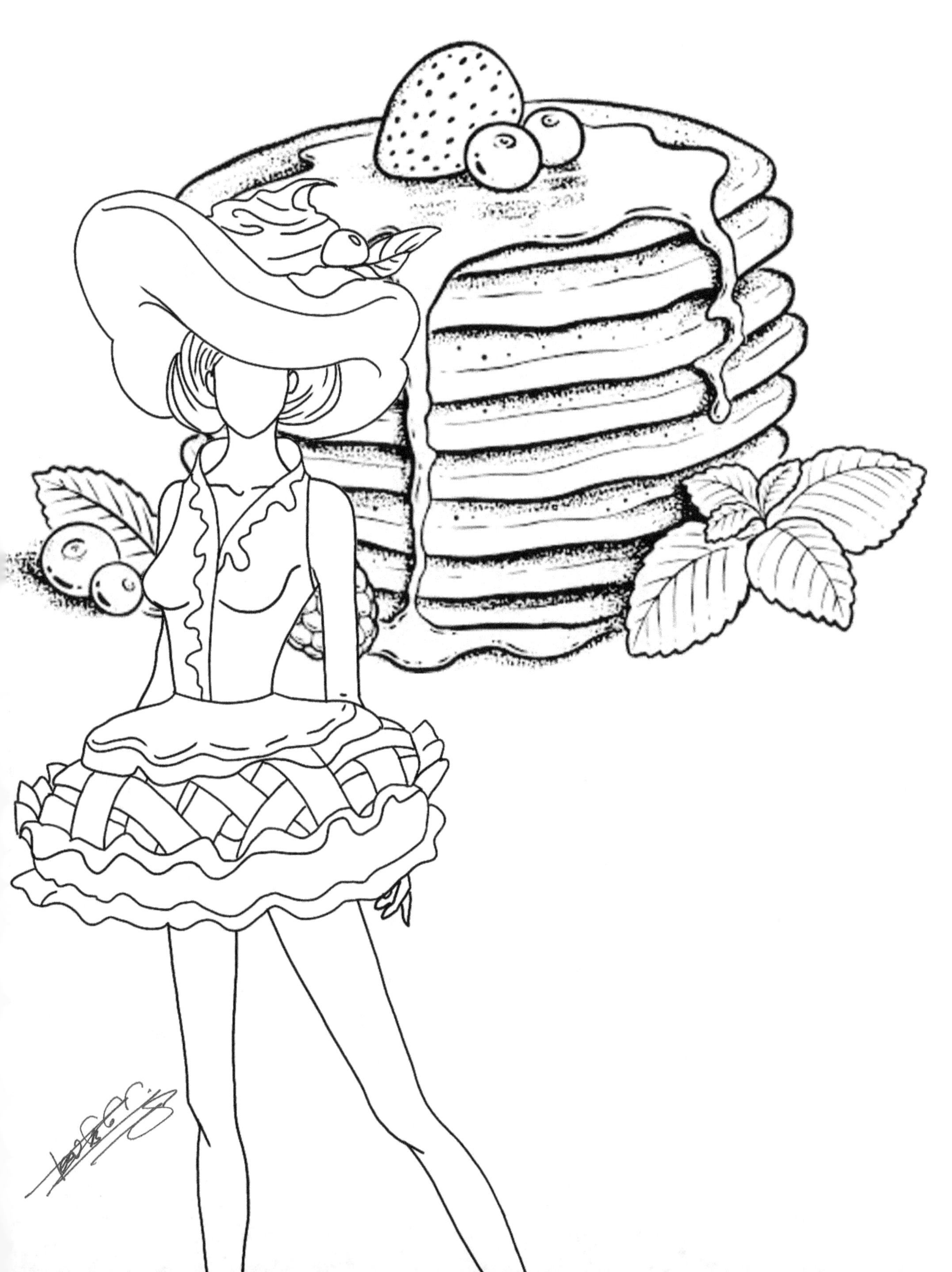

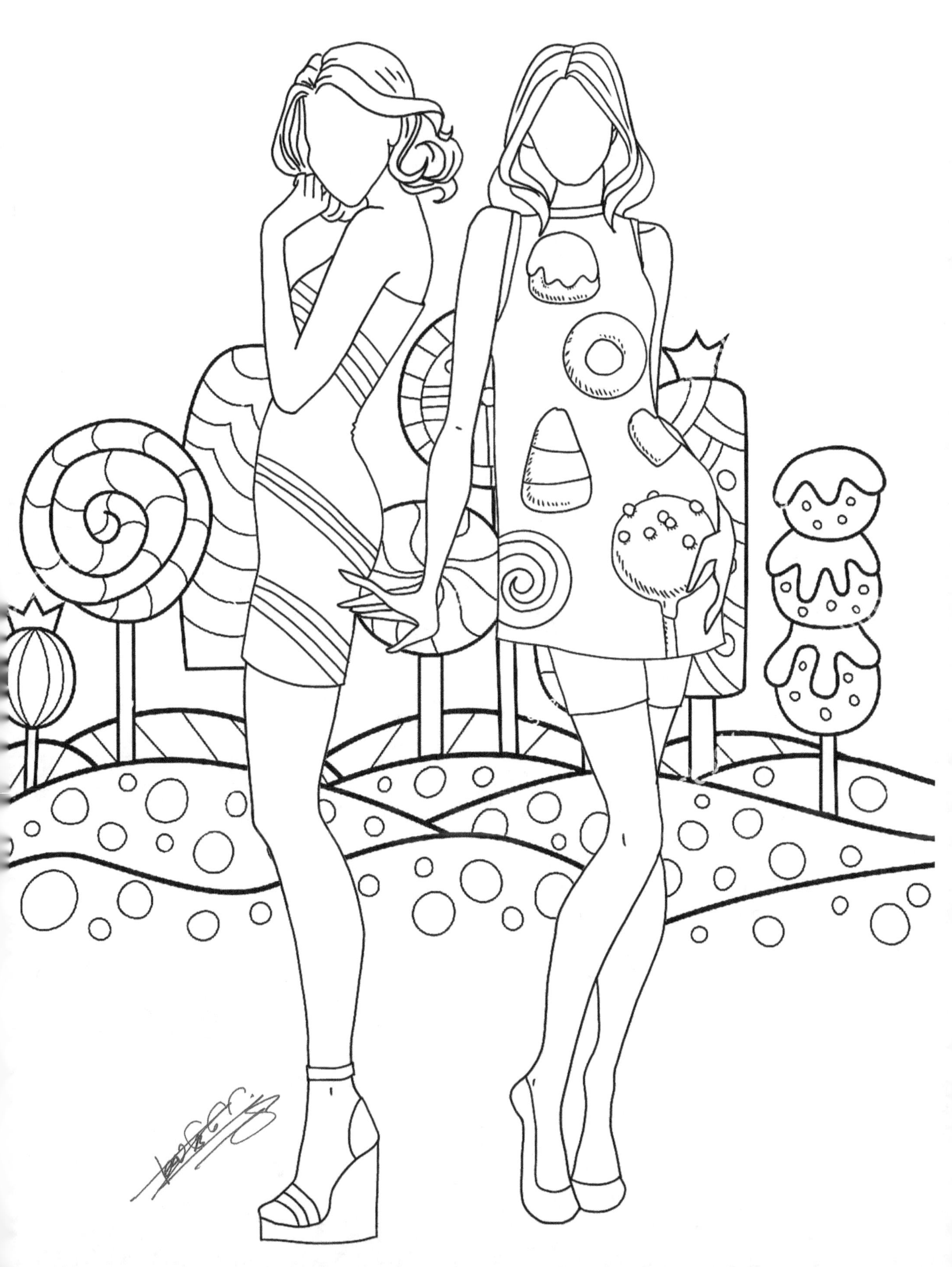

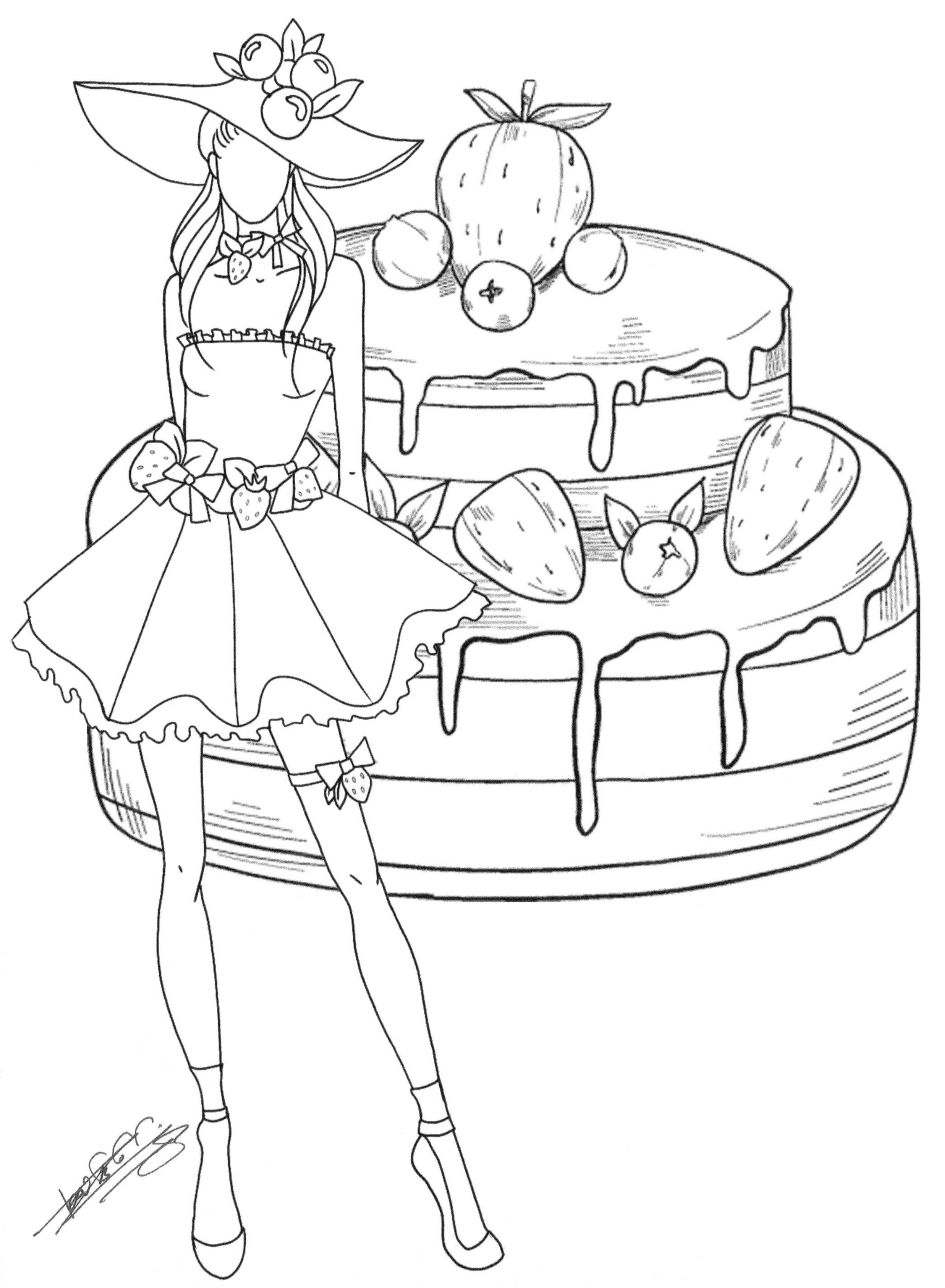

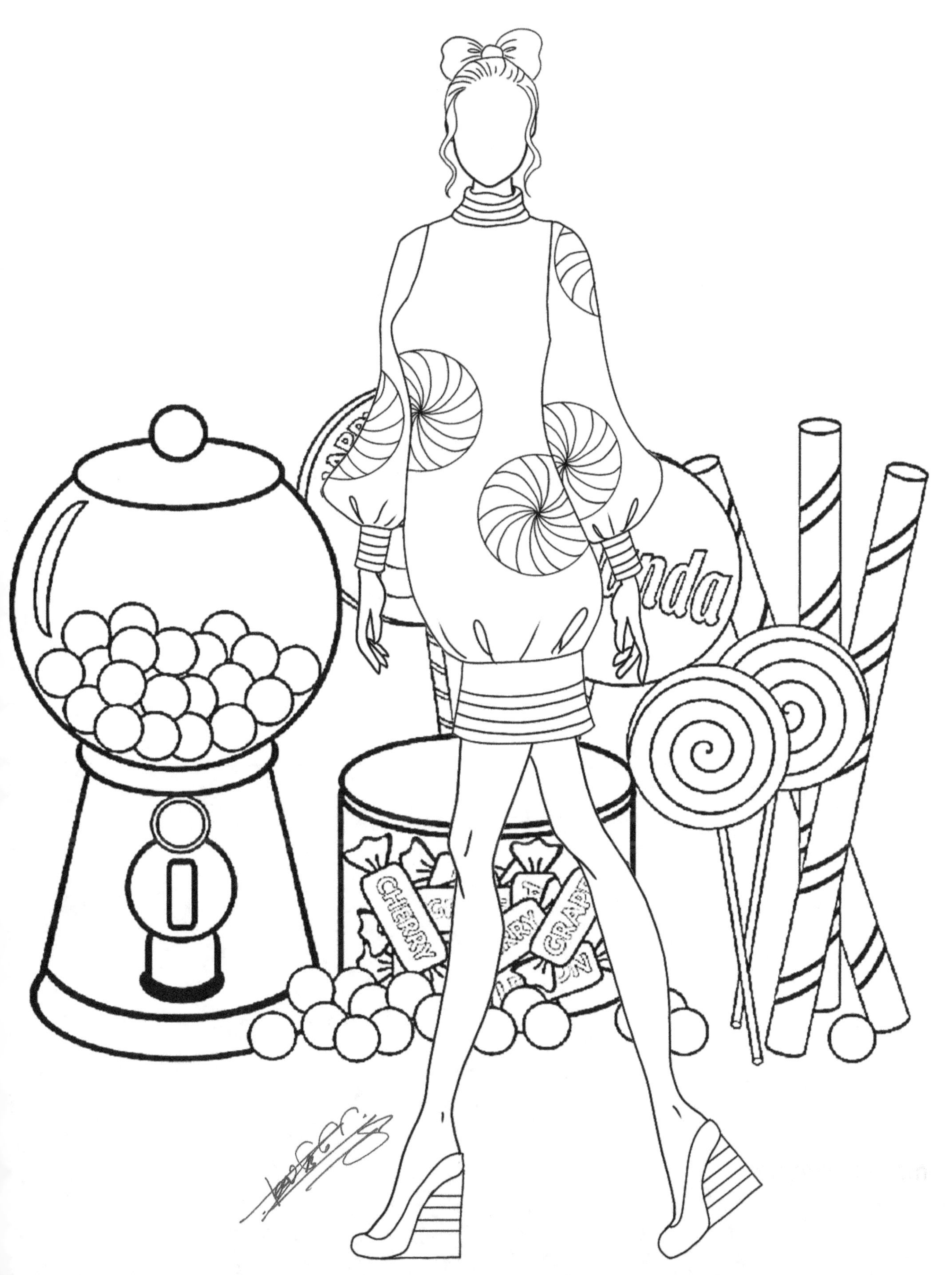

CHERRY
GRAPE
nda

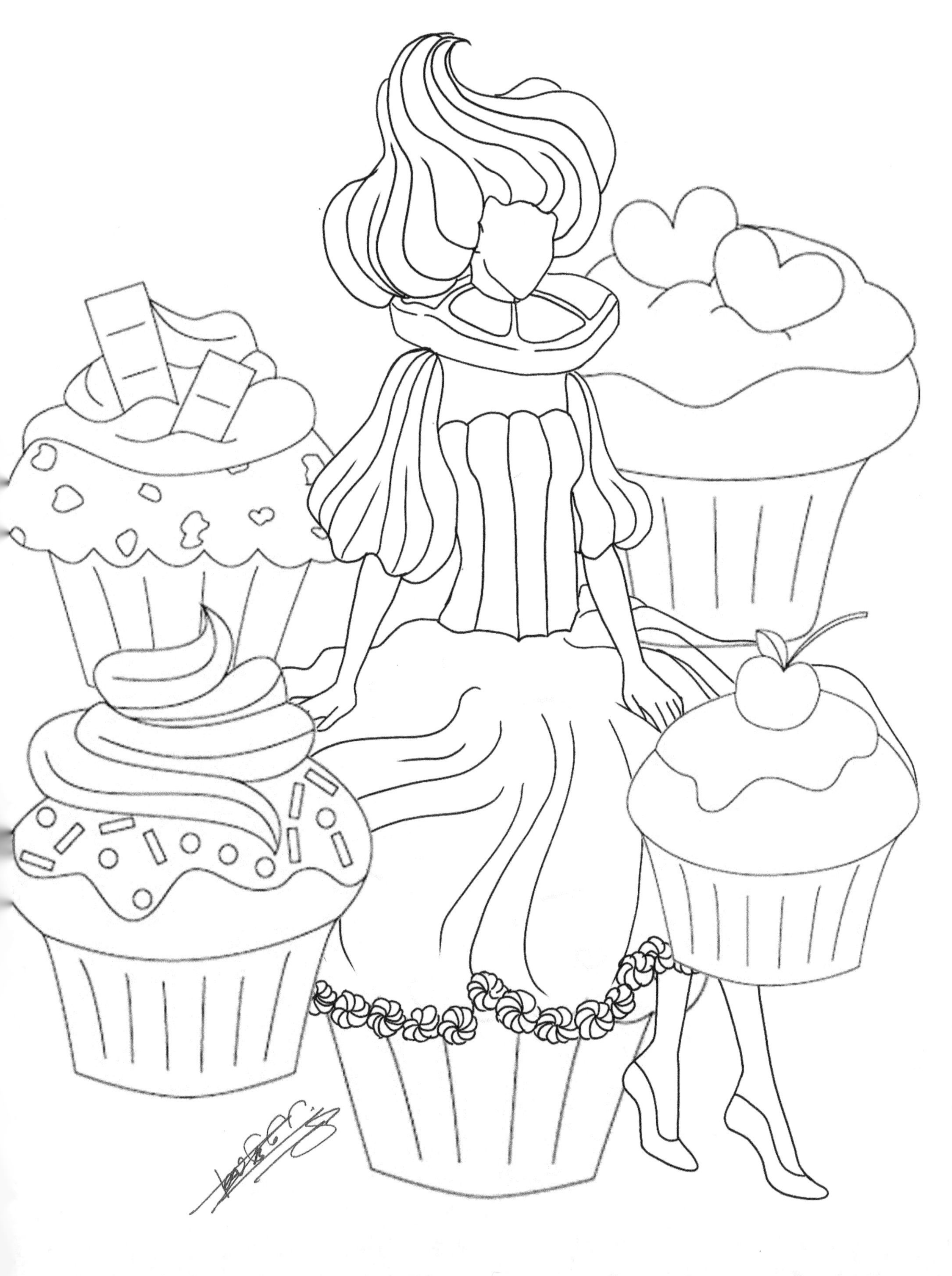

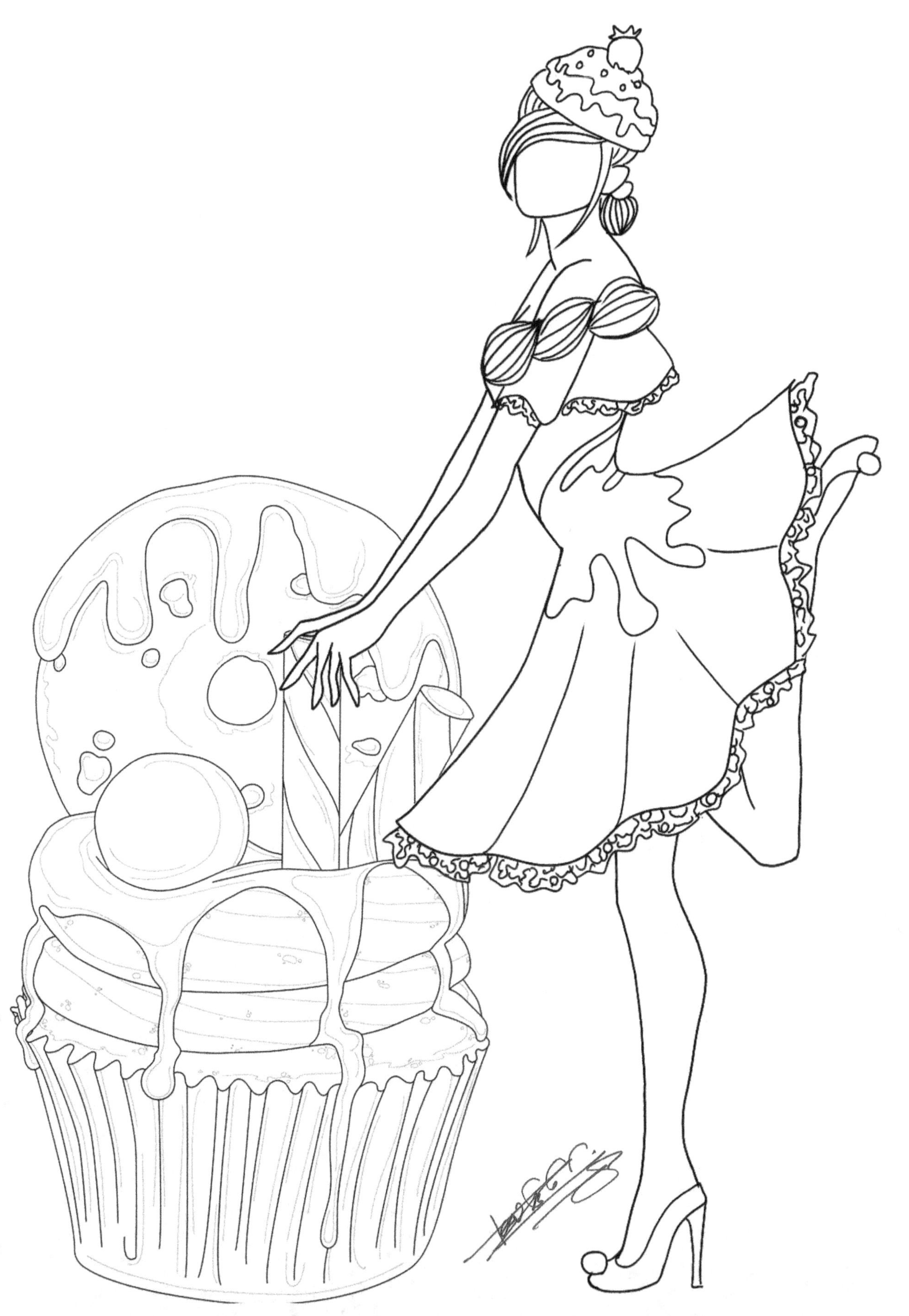

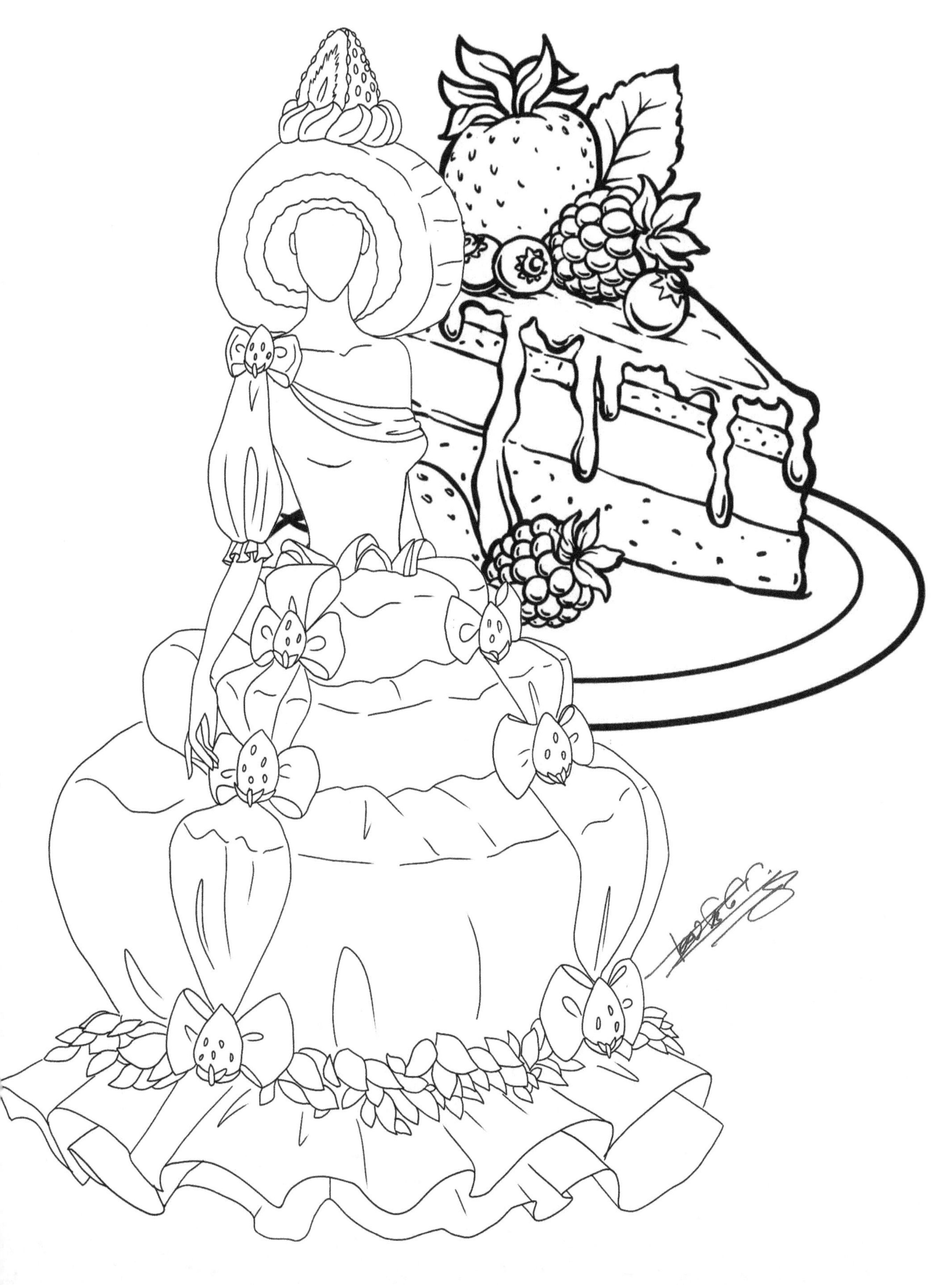

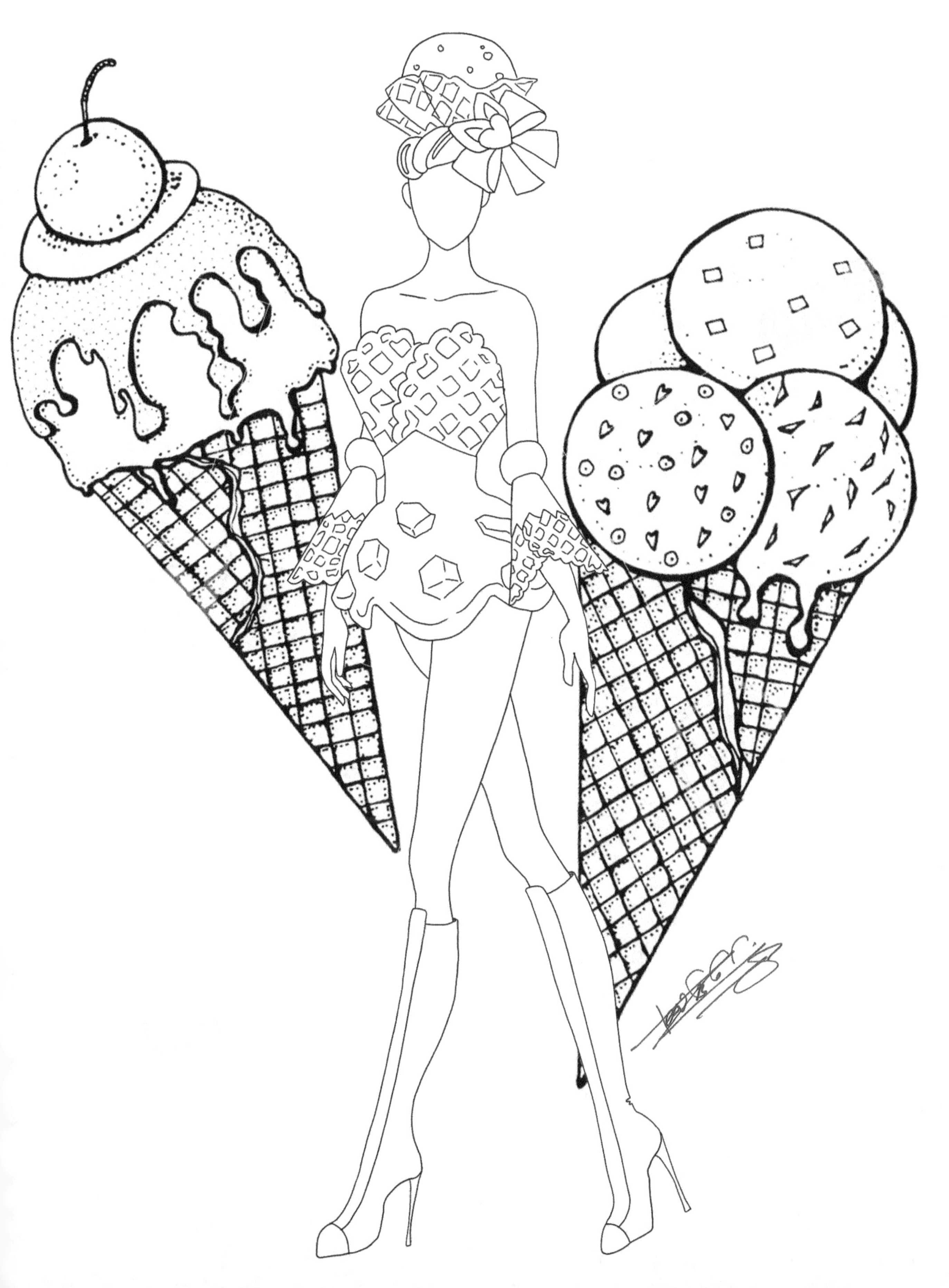

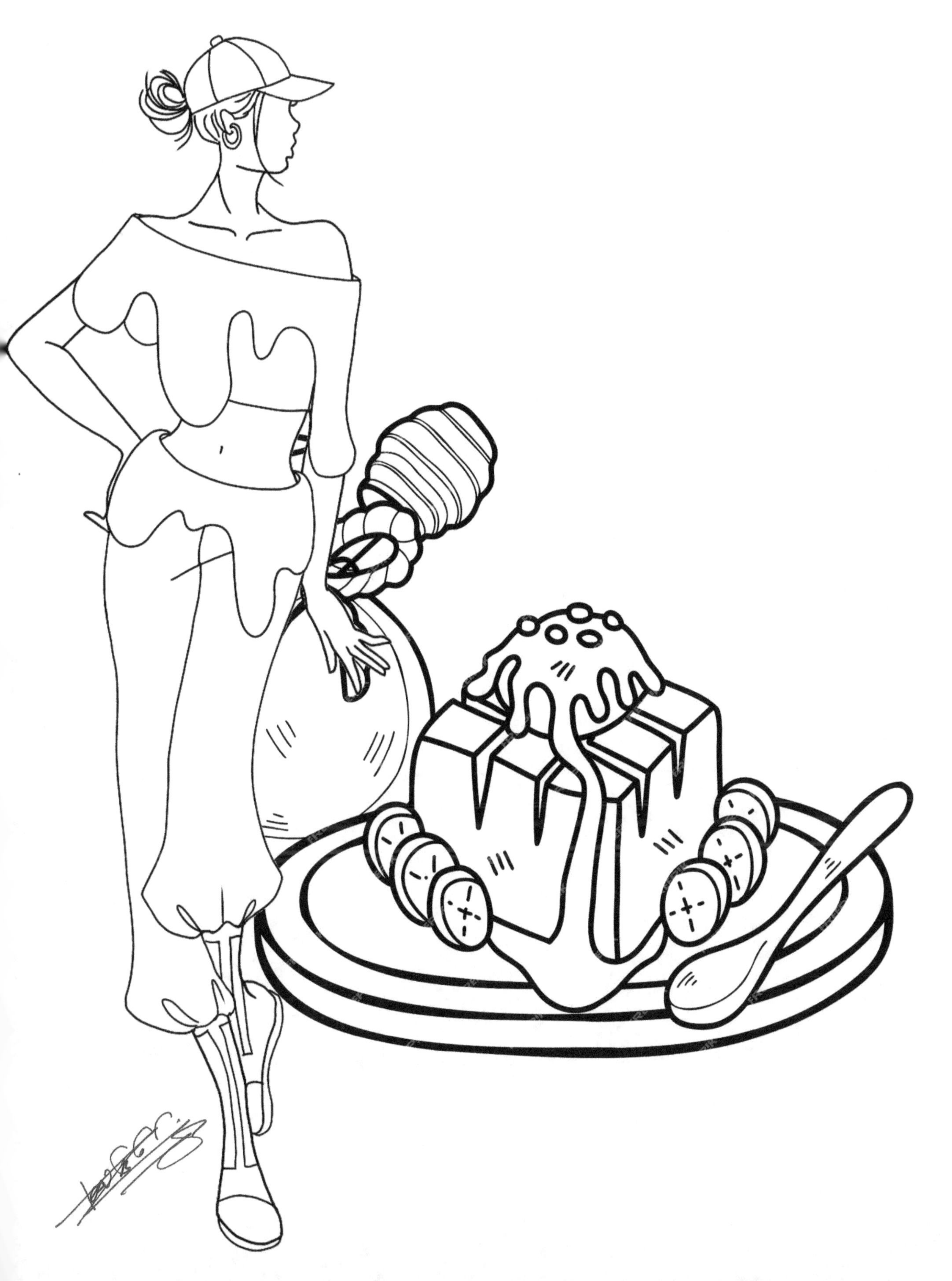

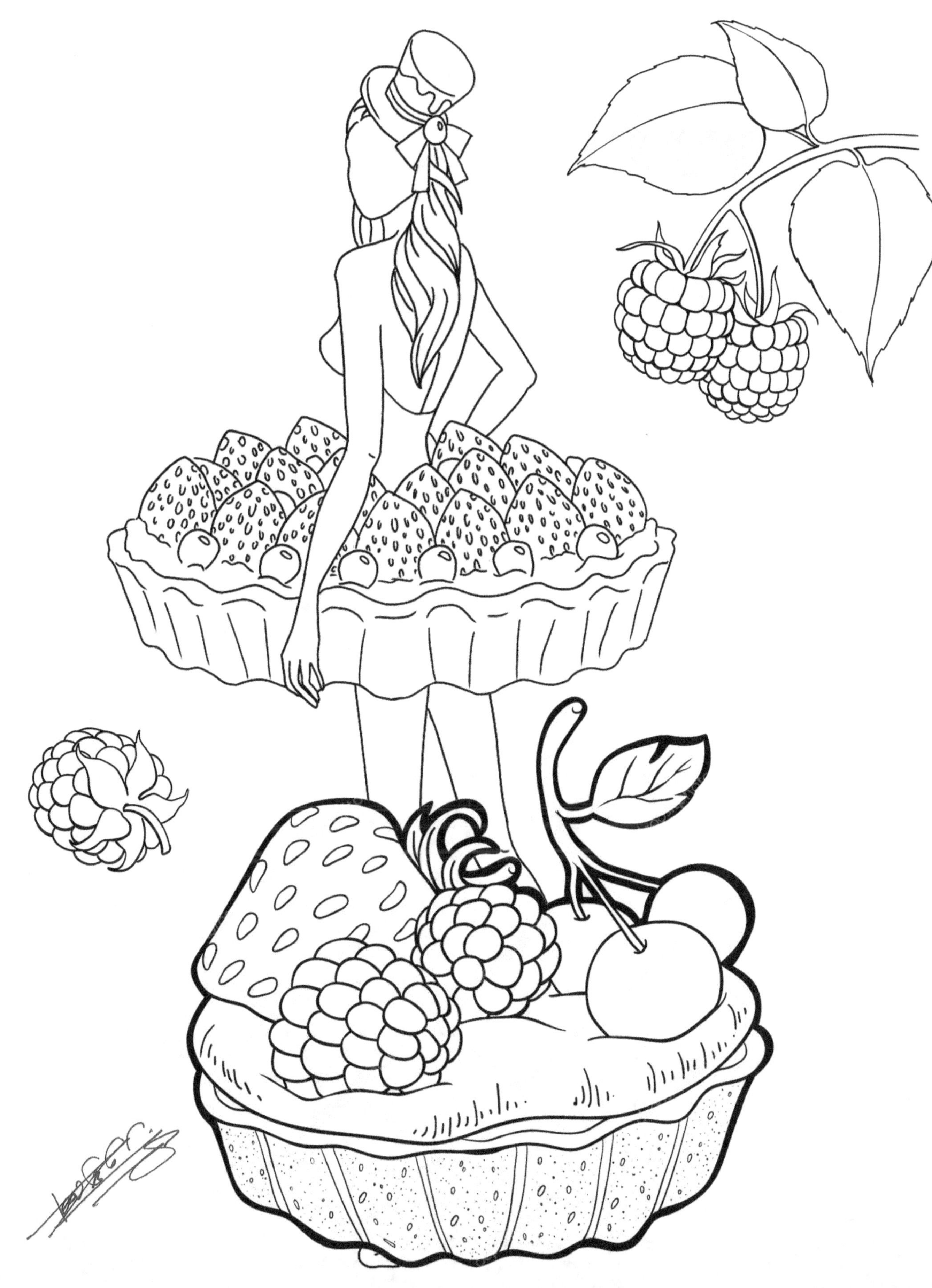

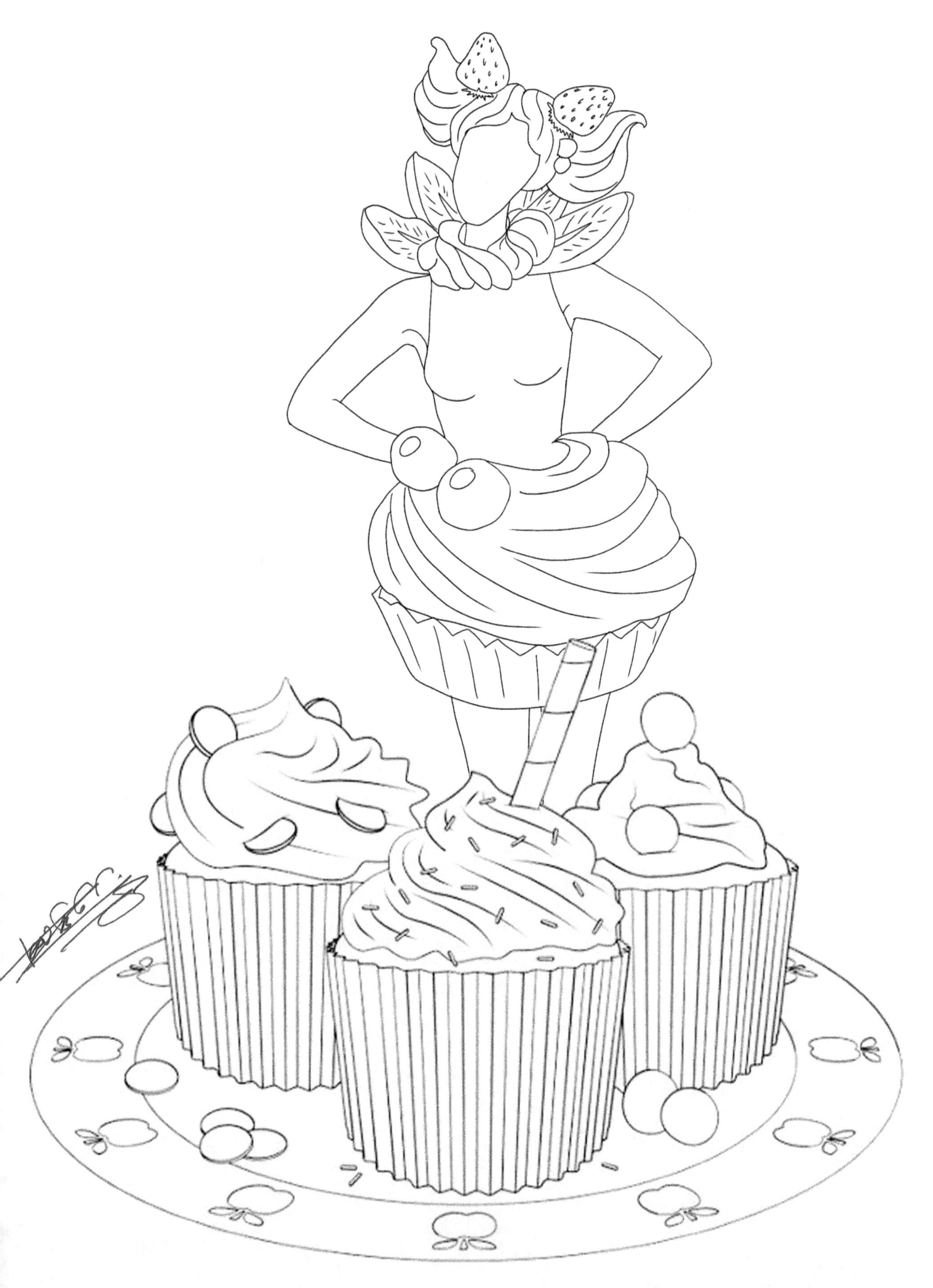

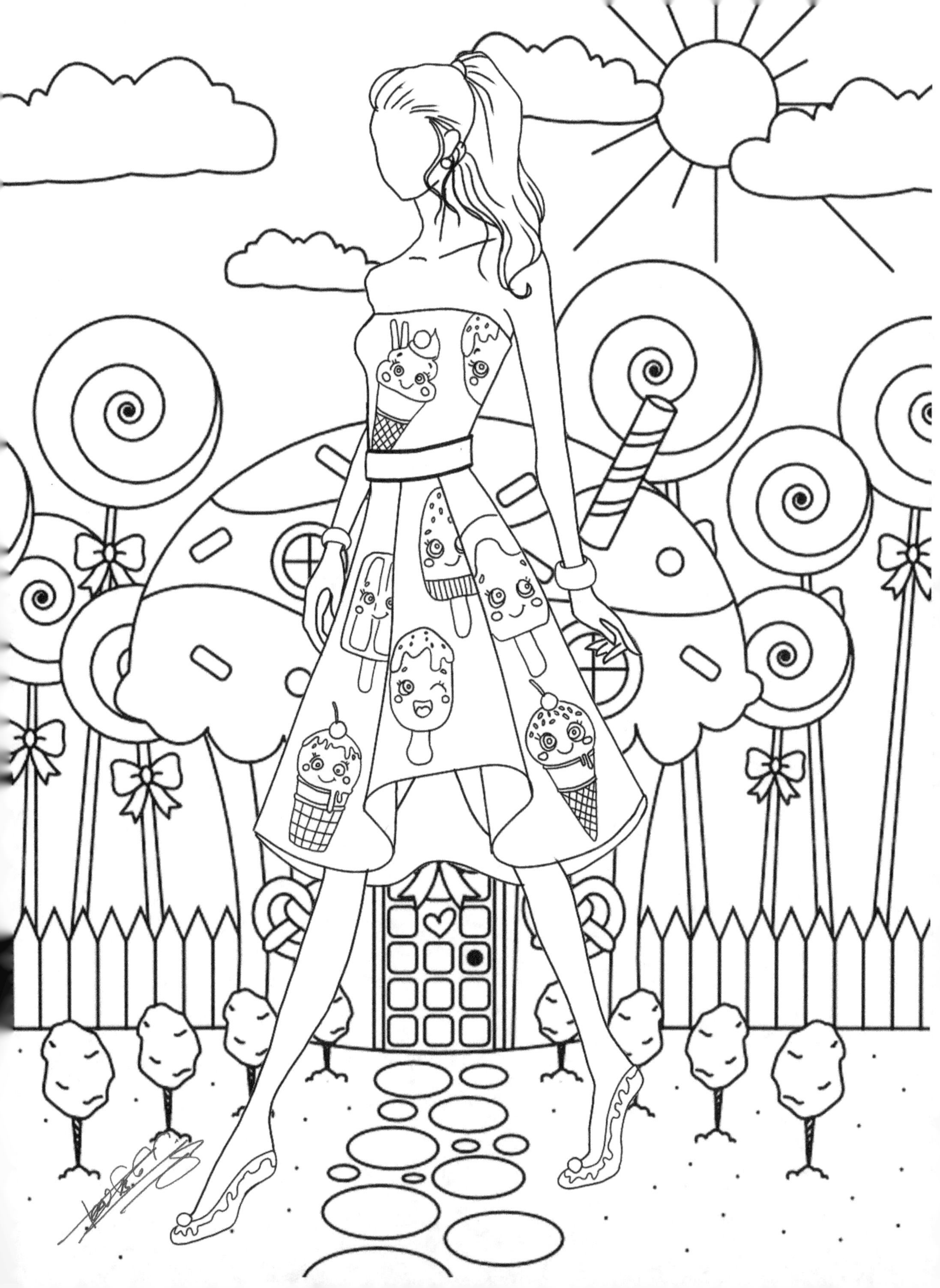

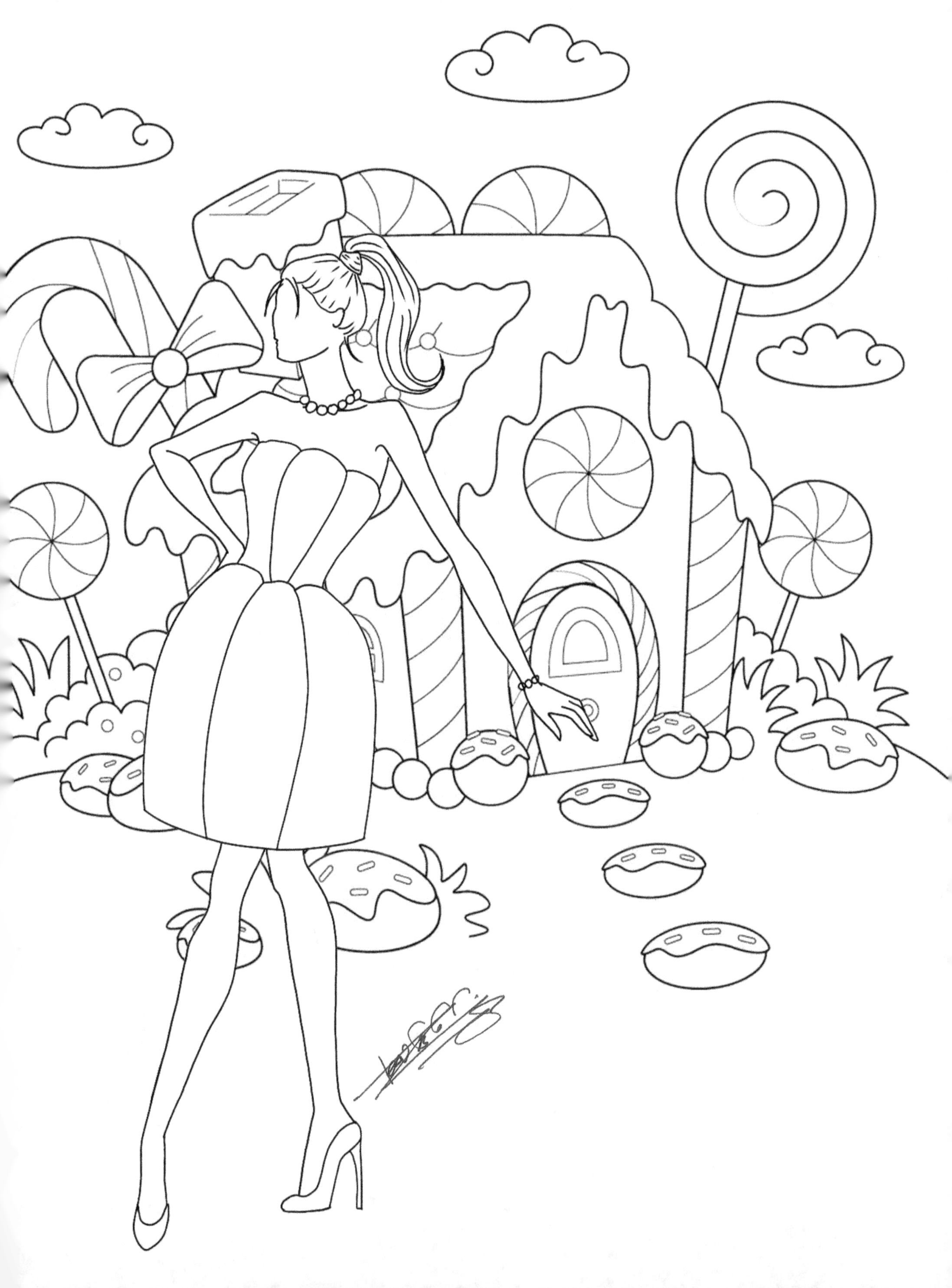

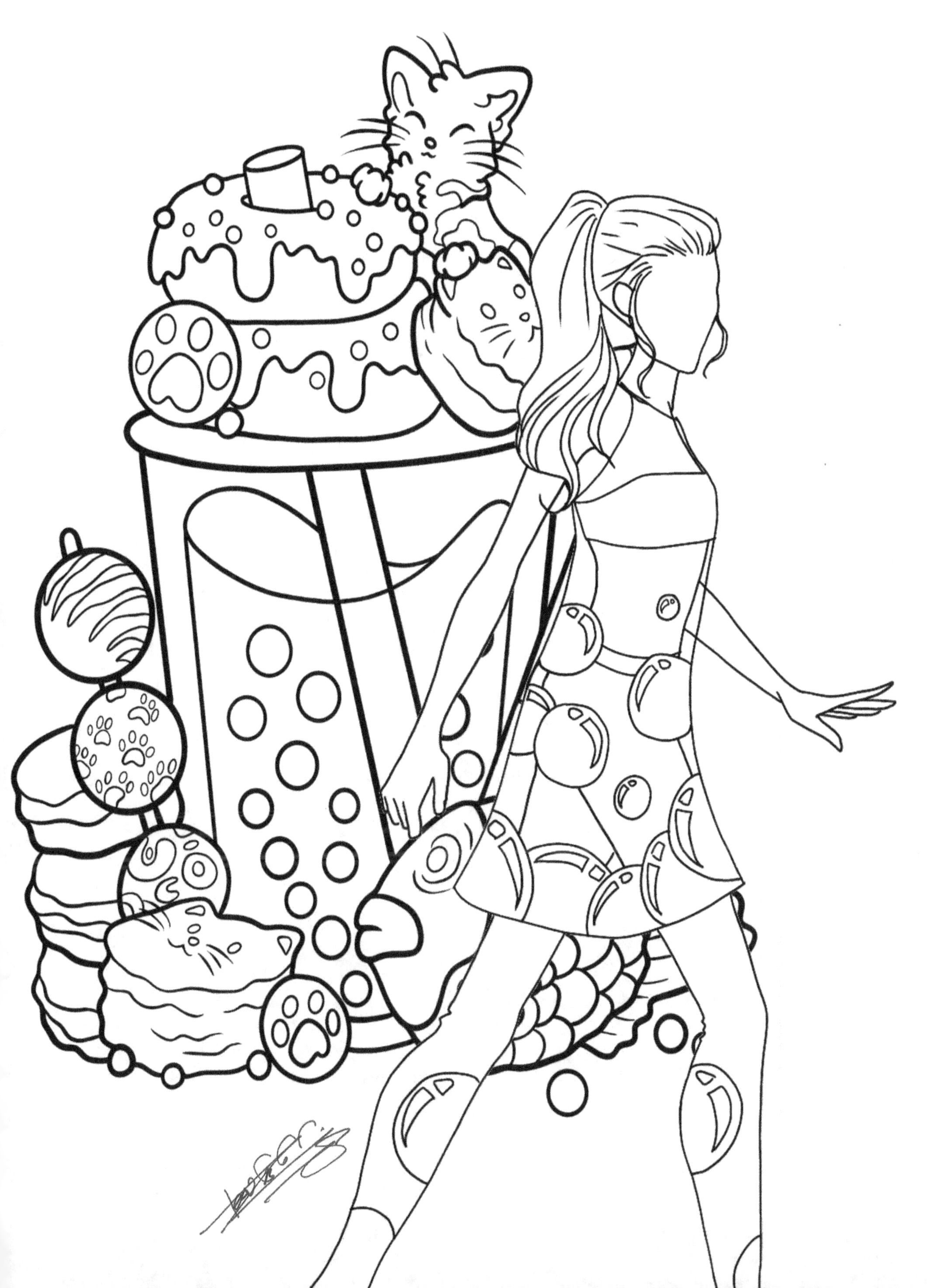

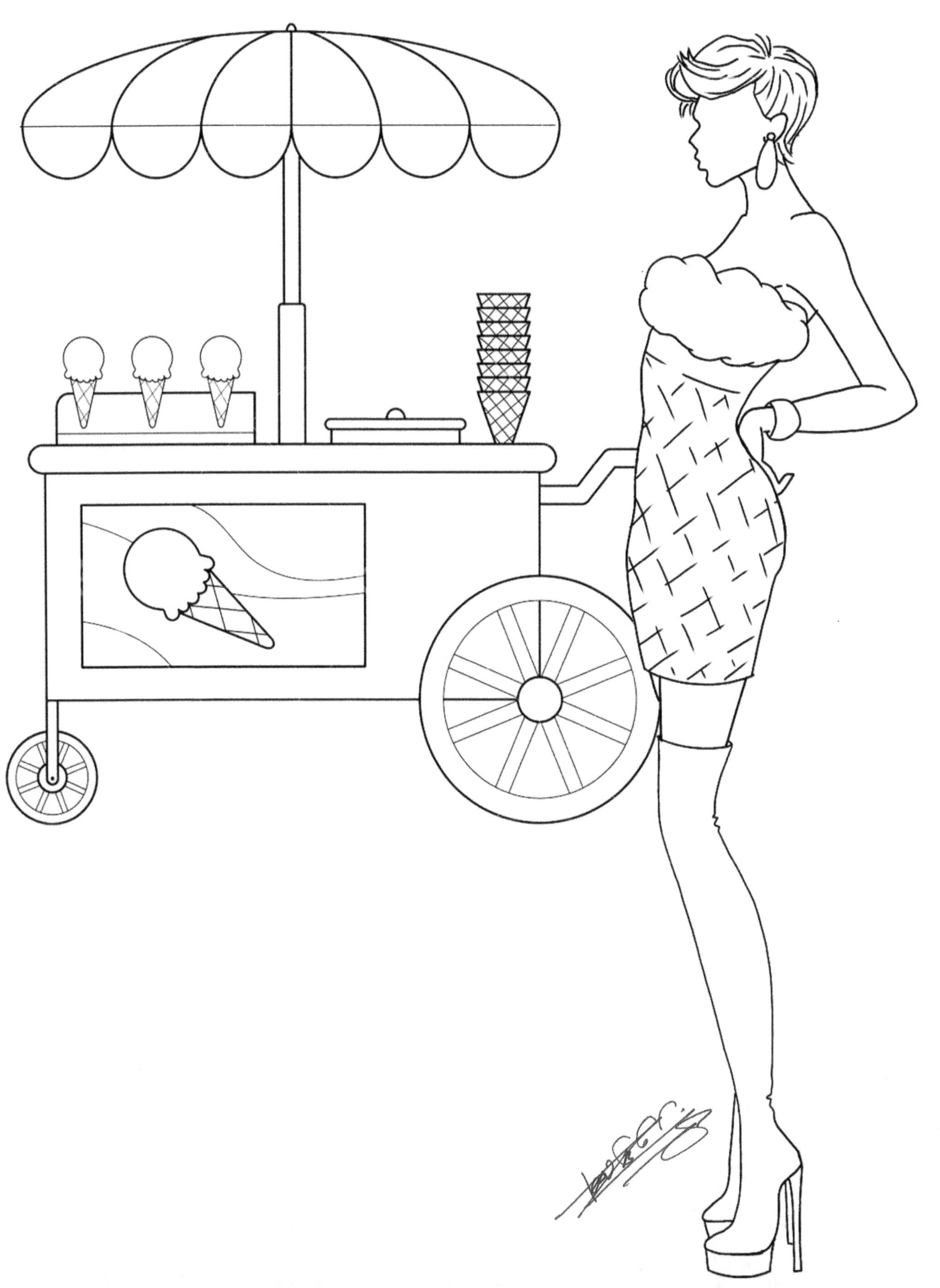

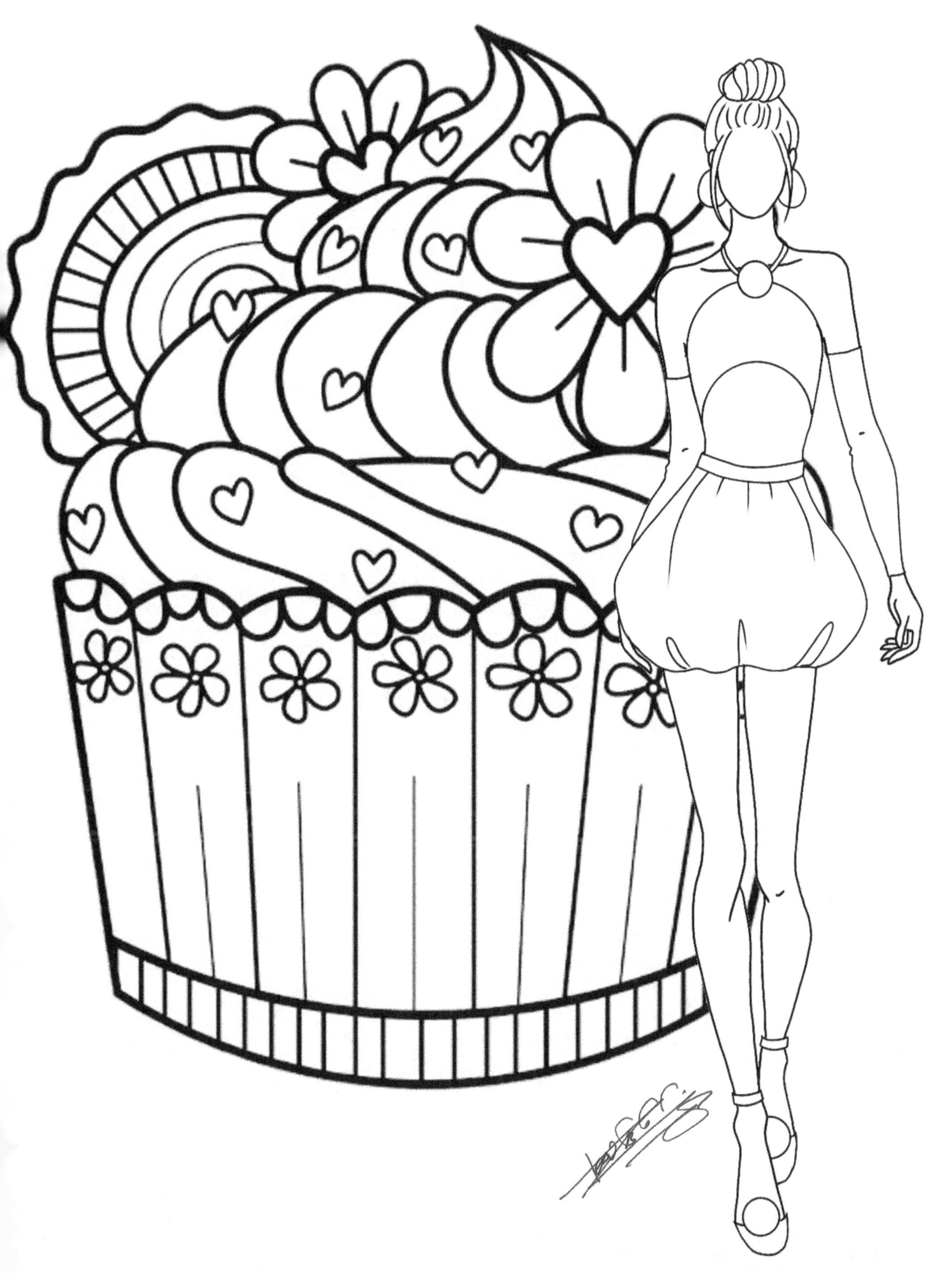

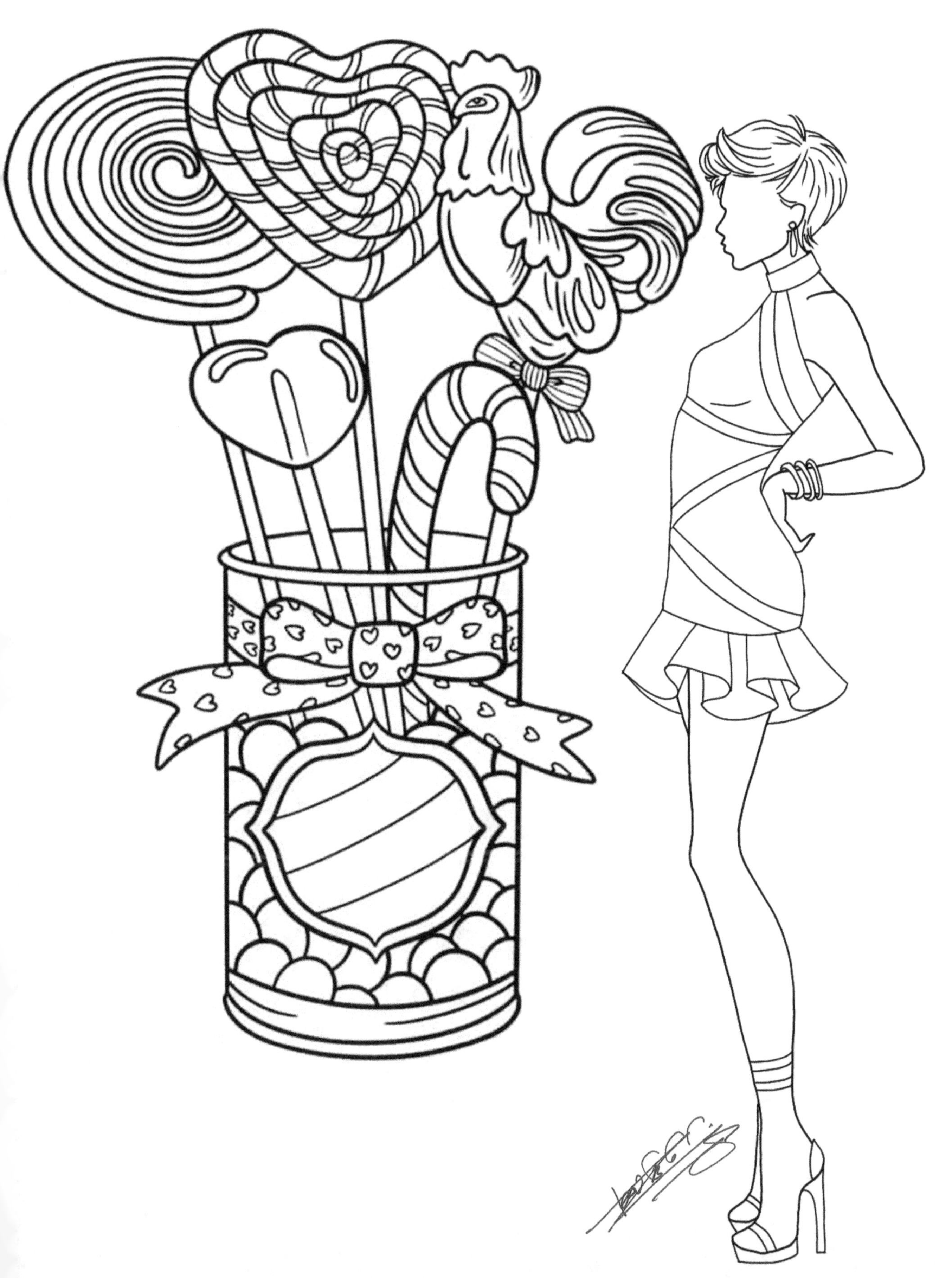

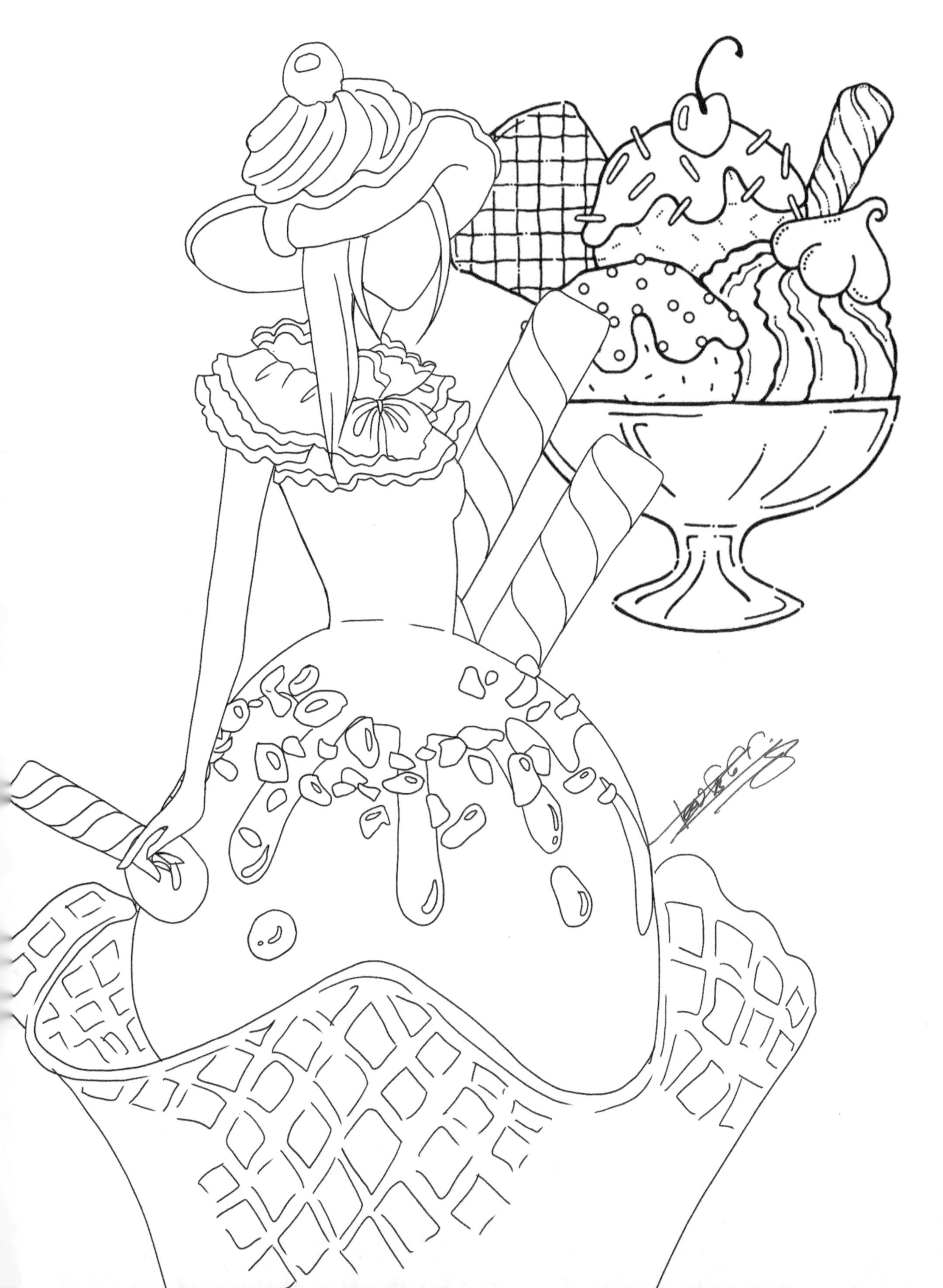

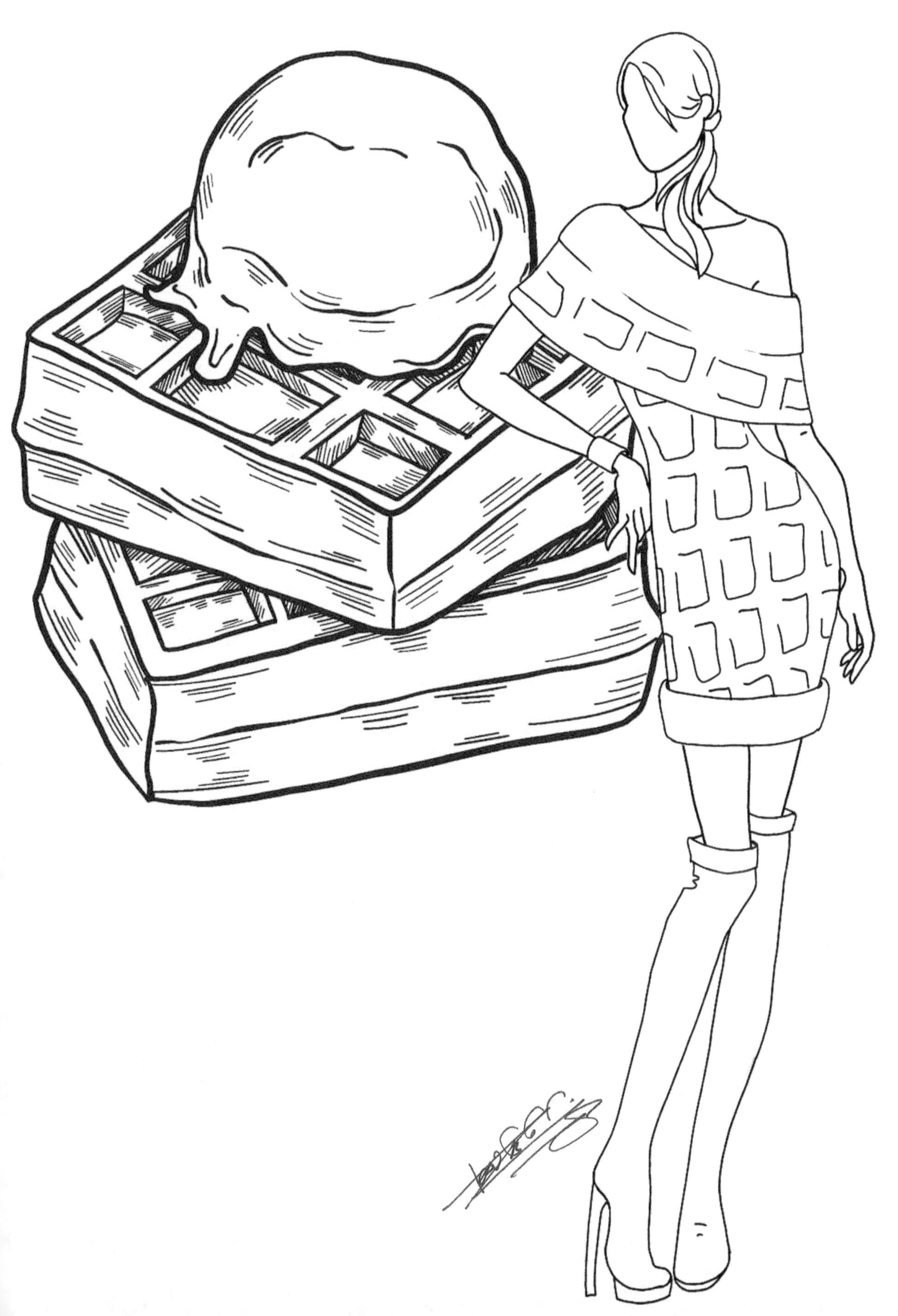

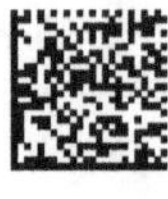